HOW TO PINCH A PENNY TILL IT SCREAMS

STRETCHING YOUR DOLLAR$ IN THE 90's

D0063594

ROCHELLE LaMOTTE McDONALD

Avery Publishing Group

Garden City Park, New York

Cover designers: Rudy Shur and Marty Hochberg
Cover painting: Rob Bolster
In-house editor: Amy C. Tecklenburg
Typesetters: Kay Rangos and William M. Gonzales
Printer: Paragon Press, Honesdale, PA

The excerpt on page 192 is from the *The American Heritage Dictionary of the English Language,* Third Edition. Copyright © 1992 by Houghton Mifflin Company. Reprinted by permission.

Library of Congress Cataloging-in-Publication Data

McDonald, Rochelle LaMotte
How to pinch a penny till it screams : stretching your dollar in the 90's / Rochelle LaMotte McDonald.
p. cm.
Includes index.
ISBN 0-89529-529-6
1. Finance, Personal. 2. Consumer education. 3. Home economics.
I. Title.
HG179.M3745 1993
332.024—dc20   93-8827
                                                                        CIP

Copyright © 1994 by Rochelle LaMotte McDonald

Printed in the United States of America.

10 9 8 7 6 5

Contents

Preface

My name is Rochelle McDonald. I'm not an expert in economics or real estate or the stock market. Like you, I'm just an average person who is trying to make my family's take-home pay stretch as far as I can. In my case, I'm doing the best I can with our limited income for my husband, our three children, and myself.

In high school, I was just an average math student, and I don't have a college degree. But I did survive six years of military life and five moves in the first three years of my marriage. Frequent moves can empty a bank account and build up the balance on credit cards quickly, if you're not careful. When my enlistment in the military ended, my husband remained in the service, and for a long time I couldn't find a job because of job shortages on base, my pregnancies, and the constant moving. If I hadn't been able to stretch my husband's paycheck, we would have drowned in a sea of debt early in our marriage.

Somehow my math skills always seem to improve miraculously when a dollar sign is placed in front of the numbers. Perhaps that's because my parents taught my brothers and sister and me to appreciate a good challenge and to make the most of what we had. My parents couldn't afford to buy all four of us everything we wanted. If we

wanted something special and/or expensive while we were
growing up, we were encouraged to earn the money to buy
it ourselves. This policy made certain that we really wanted the desired item, and we always appreciated it more
because we earned it.

Our ancestors had to be resourceful and economical
to survive. As our nation has grown and we have become
more affluent, we have forgotten many basic survival skills.
It seems to me that one of the main qualities lacking in so
many people is a fundamental curiosity about the world
around us. Perhaps it's partly from watching years of television, but many people nowadays seem content to be pas-
sive rather than to actively question and *do*. I like to cook,
read, do refunding, do needlework, or just *do something
different and interesting*—and to ask a lot of questions
about almost anything new. I'm always interested when
it comes to learning new ideas, new ways of doing things,
and especially new ways to save money. All of these interests have helped me learn to be an economical consumer
and to get the most for my money.

One of my friends once said that she thought I could
pinch a penny till it screamed and that I should write a
book about it. My husband and parents agreed. Before I
started looking for a publisher, I gave various friends a
single chapter to critique for me. Their response was
encouraging. This book is a compilation of my personal
knowledge and experience, as well as ideas from friends
and family. I have tried to touch on the chief issues that
affect our economic lives the most: food, clothing, housing,
energy, communication, transportation, leisure activities,
and health care. The suggestions contained here won't help
you get rich quick, but they may help you stay ahead of
the game. Not every idea is for everyone, but I hope this

book provides food for thought and helpful ways to save money for anyone who reads it.

While I have shared with you many of my money-saving hints, by no means am I suggesting that I hold a monopoly on the secrets to economic survival. Quite to the contrary, more than anything else I hope that this message comes across loud and clear: This is what has worked for me; you must take charge of your own economic situation. Use whatever means works for you—whether it is prayer and faith, imagination and creativity, diligence and organizational skills, or flexibility and willingness to learn new ideas and techniques—to survive economically, and to make a better life for yourself and for those around you. But whatever strategy you choose, by pinching pennies now you can create a better future for yourself and for your loved ones.

President Clinton has called upon all Americans to make a contribution toward our country's economic future. It appears that more tough economic times loom ahead. Our future as a nation might very well depend on the ability of individuals—like you and me—to relearn the importance of self-reliance and adaptability in meeting new challenges. So we now have an opportunity to do something for ourselves and for our country at the same time. We have the potential to improve the quality of our lives, and the quality of our children's lives, by fully utilizing human initiative and imagination to save our personal and national resources. Won't you join me?

1

Guidelines for Survival

You may look at the twelve guidelines below and think, "These suggestions are so obvious, I could have written this book." You're right, of course, but the very obvious things are often the most overlooked. For example, when I studied electronics, one of my instructors told the class to first make sure a machine was plugged in and turned on before we tried to diagnose a problem. You would be surprised how frequently the solution to a problem is as simple, and as apparent, as that.

Quite often, our own "machine" isn't plugged in. Or perhaps it's just not operating at full power. Whatever the reason, we frequently ignore the most basic resource available to us all—the capacity of our own minds. Give the following general guidelines some thought, for they are the key to making all the other suggestions in this book work for you. More importantly, though, these guidelines set forth principles that are fundamental to success in any of life's endeavors.

1. Be prepared to change your attitude when necessary. "You get what you pay for." "The most expensive is always the best." "Why make it when I can buy it?" "Coupons save you only a few cents." These are attitudes that can be very expensive. Every penny adds up, and sometimes you need to stretch your money further than at other times. Flexibility, or the willingness to change your attitude as conditions demand, is probably the most important guideline of all.

2. Use your imagination. Almost as important as flexibility is creativity. And don't let anyone tell you that you don't have any imagination. Everyone has some, but many people refuse to exercise it. The fact that you are reading this book is proof that you are open to new suggestions. Take what you read here, apply your imagination to look at the problem from different angles, and then build your own personal survival strategy—based on what works for *you*. Remember, often the solutions to our problems are right in front of us, but we just don't recognize them.

3. Be informed. Educate yourself. You can't make a wise decision if you don't understand your choices. No matter how old you are and no matter how much education you may have, there are always areas in which you can improve your knowledge. A Ph.D. in math might not recognize a good buy in vacuum cleaners any more than a young, newly married couple would. We all must be willing to explore and learn. First find a good source of the information you need. Then do your homework. Just knowing the right terminology for your situation can put you in a position to get a better deal than you would if you didn't seem to understand the language that's being used. And think of the money you could have saved over the years if you had only learned about this product or that service *before* you paid too much for it.

4. Talk to other people. Socializing and networking are just different names for exchanging information with other people. Whether you're at work, meeting your friends, or shopping for yourself or your family, your goal is the same: Expand your horizons and learn something new today from other people. This is especially helpful when you move to a new place, or when you are traveling. Whenever I find myself in an unfamiliar location for any length of time, I make a point of finding out as soon as possible where all the highest quality, lowest priced stores and restaurants are.

5. Organize yourself. You may not be the neatest person in the world, but if you organize your affairs, you can save a lot of time and money. Knowing where your important papers are, budgeting, planning your meals, mapping out your errands to save gas, making lists, using coupons, and practically every other money-saving tactic requires good organizational skills. Even if you have never been well organized before, cheer up! It's not that difficult. I've managed to become organized, and so can you.

6. Ask questions and never assume anything. If you don't understand something, ask. Don't let your pride get in your way. Salespeople are usually prepared to respond to most questions a consumer might ask, and the conscientious salesperson who doesn't know the answer will make every effort to find it. It's your money, and you have a right to know what you're spending it on. Always read all the small print before you sign anything. If something is promised verbally, make sure to get it in writing. Remember—the only dumb question is the one you don't ask.

7. Ask yourself: Is it practical? Everybody else has one. So what? Peer pressure, fads, and trends can all become very expensive. If the product is just going to end up sitting in your closet or cupboard, it's not really worth the money. Do you really *need* a second VCR, when all the first one does is sit on top of your television, blinking to remind you how inept you are at using it? Give yourself a day or so to consider how often you would actually use the item—be honest—and then buy it *only* if you really need it.

8. Use common sense. Can you make a particular product yourself for less than the store's price? Do you have the skill to change that light fixture or fix that leaky faucet, or do you need an electrician or plumber to do it for you? First, evaluate the need and see if your resources are sufficient to handle it. If not, perhaps another member of the family, or a friend, has the expertise required. On the other hand, if the job really is too big for you to handle by yourself, by all means get more experienced help. Don't be too proud to admit that a job is out of your league. If it is, hiring professional help in the first place can save you money in the long run.

9. Shop around. Fight the urge to buy the first item you see. It's often possible to save a few hundred dollars, or even more, on a major purchase by shopping around. If you're in the market for a major purchase but don't need it right away, keep your eyes open and comparison shop when you're out. That way, you'll know what the price range is in your area and you'll be prepared to take advantage of any special deal you might find. I've actually seen the price for some items drop during the period when I was shopping around. Of course, it doesn't happen all the time, but saving a substantial amount of money makes the waiting worthwhile. On the other hand, it's foolish to drive all over town and waste gas just to save a few cents on a small purchase. Also, buy as close to the source as possible, cutting out the middlemen who add to the cost of the product. Buying "wholesale" should mean that there are fewer middlemen, but don't just assume that because it's sold directly, it always costs less. The only way to be sure is to compare prices.

10. Don't allow yourself to be pressured. Resist the power of suggestion. Salesmen and advertising agencies are paid to make you want to buy something—that's their job. Your "job" is to buy only what you really want and to secure the best price under the circumstances. Have you ever seen that nice juicy orange or that thick, sizzling steak on television and suddenly felt hungry? How often have you bought something that was displayed attractively at the end of the supermarket aisle, or that you sampled at a store—even though it wasn't on your shopping list? That sudden feeling that you need this product *now*, when you hadn't given it a second thought before, shows the power of suggestion. I've modified my attitude to accept the fact that I can't get everything I want right now. As a result, instead of feeling deprived, I feel free to take my time and evaluate exactly what the product or service is worth *to me*. I'll usually purchase an item when I need it but not before, and certainly not when *someone else* wants me to buy.

11. If it doesn't feel right, don't do it. If a product or service is really a bargain, and if the company or individual selling it is reputable, you will be given time to make your decision. If the deal sounds "too good to be true" or "too good to pass up," you definitely should give it more time.

12. Learn when to say no. After you have investigated the price and thought about your needs, if you decide you really don't need or can't afford an item, say no and stick to it. If you give in and buy something you can't afford, will you really be able to enjoy the item, considering the guilt and stress the debt will produce? Wouldn't you rather wait until you can afford it with a clear conscience? Saying no can be a positive step that makes you feel good about yourself, enables you to maintain healthy self-discipline, and creates a climate that will allow you to say yes when the timing and economics are right for you.

Whether you are single and trying to make it on your own, a young couple working and saving to start a family, a growing family needing to provide for its members, or an elderly person living on a fixed income, you probably need to guard your limited financial resources. What I am offering here is a commonsense guide to survival during difficult economic times. If you learn these principles and apply them well during the tough times, you will survive until the financial picture improves. Then pinching a penny will no longer hurt, and it may just feel good.

All of the suggestions in this book are designed to help you save money. Some, of course, will save you more than others—but they are all important because every penny you save adds up. Keep that principle in mind as you read the chapters that follow, and use my "three-penny scale":

 *Three pennies indicates an idea that can save a really substantial amount of money.*

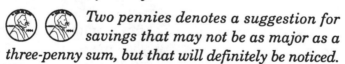 *Two pennies denotes a suggestion for savings that may not be as major as a three-penny sum, but that will definitely be noticed.*

One penny marks an idea that saves a small to moderate amount of money—you may not think it looks like much by itself, but when you add it to your other pennies, or let it build up over time, you'll be surprised how much you can save!

2

Managing Your Money

Many people face financial problems at one time or another, because of inflation, a temporary decrease in income, unexpected expenses, or unemployment. These problems are sometimes unavoidable, but fortunately they don't usually last very long. On the other hand, you may be one of those individuals who can't quite manage your money over the long term. You have trouble saying no to purchases; you get overextended on your credit cards and have to deal with a negative balance in your checking account. You may even find yourself borrowing more money from other sources to pay off your existing debts. While sometimes it can make sense to borrow money to consolidate your debts, usually this doesn't do anything more than lead you into further difficulty, which causes even more worry and stress.

These problems can be overcome, however, if you learn how to use your resources wisely. It's best to avoid the debt trap in the first place by learning to manage money as early in your life as possible. But it's never too late to begin.

I look at personal finance as having four parts: spending, budgeting, saving, and credit. These are all related, of course, and in a sense the last three are all different aspects of managing your spending.

SPENDING

Who doesn't know how to spend? Most of us enjoy buying new things, whether they are for us personally or for someone else, whether they are practical items to help out around the house or that luxury purchase we have been dreaming about. Sometimes the very activity of shopping, searching for just the right service or product, can even be fun and entertaining. Unfortunately, what many people *don't* know is how to spend wisely. This book is filled with ideas on that subject, so I will not go into more detail here, except to point out a number of basic principles to keep in mind whenever you spend money for any product or service.

Perhaps the most important step you can take is to make yourself aware of your rights as a consumer. By being aware of your rights and taking a few precautions *before* you have a problem with a merchant, service provider, or creditor, you can often minimize difficulties. Remember, the principle of *caveat emptor* (let the buyer beware) still applies in the marketplace; the main responsibility for protecting your money and your interests lies with you, the individual. Before, during, and after parting with your money, always keep in mind the following guidelines.

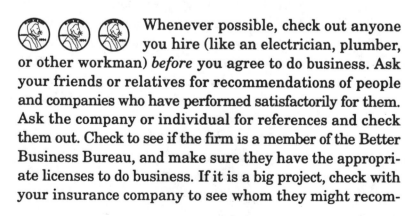 Whenever possible, check out anyone you hire (like an electrician, plumber, or other workman) *before* you agree to do business. Ask your friends or relatives for recommendations of people and companies who have performed satisfactorily for them. Ask the company or individual for references and check them out. Check to see if the firm is a member of the Better Business Bureau, and make sure they have the appropriate licenses to do business. If it is a big project, check with your insurance company to see whom they might recom-

mend. These steps can save you much time, money, and aggravation later.

Get everything in writing. Don't take a verbal agreement for granted. If you have any questions, ask them now—before you run into problems.

When shopping around, always ask about guarantees or warranties. Some warranties cover only parts, not labor; keep in mind that labor can be the most expensive part of a repair job. If an extended warranty is available, make sure you understand exactly what it covers, when coverage begins and ends, and how much it costs. In many cases, you can wind up paying more for an extended warranty than it would cost to replace a product with a new one. Look at buying an extended warranty just as you would look at any other purchase. Remember, salespeople are trained to promote extended warranties because of the high profits involved, not because they are doing you a favor.

Very often, simple things like getting and keeping receipts and warranty slips can help solve a problem. If you make a habit of always asking for a sales receipt, no matter how small the purchase, then you will always have the important ones should a problem arise. Register warranties right away, and keep copies of warranties and important receipts together in a safe place. If a product should break or prove to be defective, you can determine if it's still under warranty and might be repaired for free or for a small charge.

Try Bartering
Instead of Spending

Bartering is a way to stretch your money. Bartering doesn't usually involve an exchange of money, but it's a form of business transaction that involves the trading of goods or services. Our ancestors used this method of trade for generations, and it is being revived in the business world. It should be revived for the average person because it is an excellent way to save money and still get some of the goods and services you need.

I have a group of friends who barter successfully. None of us has much extra money, but we each specialize in something. For example, one of my friends watched my three kids one night so my husband and I could go out for a few hours as adults rather than as parents. In exchange, I cooked dinner for her. We had our night out, and she had her day out of the kitchen. I had another friend who baked lovely cakes, and I had a couple of really nice cake pans that I didn't use. I traded her the pans for a nicely decorated cake. My husband has frequently traded his muscles or knowledge with other men who needed help. If an extra man was needed for a job, my husband would lend a hand; when he needed extra hands, the men he helped would join in and help him. By pooling our talents, we stretch our dollars.

Be sure to keep track of your correspondence. Keep copies of your personal business letters for future reference, and file them together with any correspondence you receive from the other parties. If you talk to anyone on the phone about a problem, make sure to get the person's name, and note the time, date, and the essentials of the conversation.

If you aren't satisfied with a company's services or products and you want your money back, don't settle for less. If the company sends you a partial refund, don't deposit or cash the check unless there's a letter with it specifying that it is a partial payment. Otherwise, your signature on the check can be taken to indicate that you accepted it as full settlement.

Don't sign any forms that have any blank spaces. When signing purchase agreements or other forms, make sure all the blanks are filled in by writing in ink.

If you're having a problem and have tried everything you can think of to straighten it out, short of calling the authorities, call the Consumer Protection Agency, a state agency that will look into any claim you file. You can find the Consumer Protection Agency listed under "State Government" in your phone book. You also have various legal rights according to federal law. Under truth-in-lending laws, for example, you have the right to know (and the lender has the obligation to tell you) the finance charges and the annual interest rate for any money you borrow. You also have the right to cancel a transaction within three business days, Monday through Saturday, excluding Sundays and holidays.

According to the Equal Credit Opportunity Act, a credit application cannot ask for information about race, sex, religion, nationality, or age; nor can you be discriminated against based on these factors. If you believe you have been denied or charged excessively high rates for credit in violation of the law, you can file a complaint with the Federal Trade Commission, which will investigate.

If you are trying to make ends meet, though, remember this one important fact: When all is said and done, it is always easier to spend less than it is to earn more. And because of income taxes, spending ten dollars less on a purchase is actually nearly twice as beneficial as earning ten dollars more. That's why the remainder of this book will show you how to *control* your spending, which is exactly what a budget can help you do.

BUDGETING

Budget is one of those words that everyone dreads to hear. For some people, it conjures up visions of a ball and chain. To me, however, it represents the ability to control my spending, which frees me from the stress of financial uncertainty. My budget makes me the master of the household money; it doesn't master me!

Most people would not think of starting out on a long trip across the country without a map or some other kind of plan, and hopefully neither would you. After all, you certainly don't need to get lost. A budget is like a road map for your financial future. It is nothing more than a plan, a way of determining how you will make it financially from one month to the next, and from one year to the next, so that you can arrive where you would like to be, on time, and in good financial shape.

Identify Your Goals

The very first step in financial planning is to establish your personal and collective goals: Where do you want to go, financially, and how long do you want the trip to be? For example, do you want to own your own home by age thirty? Are you planning to have children? Is it one of your goals to be financially independent by middle age? Will you want to send your children to college? When will you be able to retire? The answers to these questions, and to others like them, will help you plan your financial trip.

To simplify your planning, I suggest that you divide your goals into three categories, based on the time frame in which you hope to accomplish them: categories like *now* (six months or less in the future), *worth waiting for* (one to five years in the future), and *make it happen* (more than five years in the future). It is very easy to get caught up in the pressing needs of everyday living and to neglect your future; by writing down your long-term goals and consistently working to achieve them, you are more likely to keep your focus on such important objectives as a child's college education, that dream vacation, or retirement.

Develop Your Budget

You (and if you are married, your spouse) probably bring home paychecks periodically. You're probably also obligated to spend some of that money immediately, and more of it as your bills come due. Hopefully, it's not all used up right away on bills. If it is, that's a definite danger signal.

Like most people, you probably have a vague idea of how most of your money is spent, where it goes, and when the bills are due. You probably also know approximately how much your paycheck will be each pay period. Unfortunately, and again like most people, you probably *don't* have a definite plan that allows you to balance the two—income and outflow—with some fairly precise knowledge *in advance* of where you will be financially at the end of a certain period. When it comes to money matters, nothing could be more true than the cliche, "If you fail to plan, you plan to fail."

A budget does not have to be complicated or frightening. In fact, the simpler a budget is, the better. The starting point for any budget is to determine how much income you have, or can reasonably hope to attain, during a set period. Since most bills are calculated on a monthly basis, one month is a likely budget period; even if you are paid weekly, biweekly, or at some other interval, you may still find it easier to work out a budget based on one month. If you or your spouse has a stable income and the other has a part-time or irregularly paying job, you should base your budget on the stable income. The other paycheck can be used for extras or to make additional payments on outstanding bills. And if your pay fluctuates from period to period, simply calculate your average monthly income by adding together six consecutive checks and dividing the total by the number of months covered.

You might also have income from other sources. Interest from savings accounts, stock dividends, child support and alimony payments, social security checks, insurance payments to you, and any other income should be considered on the income side of your budget also.

The expenses side of your budget should include *all* of your normal expenditures: your house payment or rent; utilities (electricity, gas, water and sewer, telephone, garbage pickup, etc.); food expenses (don't forget to list any meals you eat out, like lunches at work); normal automobile expenses, like gas and oil; clothing for you and the family; life, health, home, auto, and other insurance payments; and anything else you pay regularly. Some expenses, such as house payments, stay the same from month to month, while others, such as utilities or credit payments, may fluctuate. After you have listed all of your expenses, it's easy to determine where your money is going, how much you should have remaining at the end of the budget period, and in what areas you might need to spend less.

Table 2.1 shows a sample budget for one month. Using this as a guide, and based on the points that follow, take some time to create a simple budget that will help you understand and control where your money goes.

Table 2.1 A Sample Budget for January

Income	Expenses	
$1,500 (Sara)	Savings (for down payment	
$1,200 (Phil)	on house)	$ 100
$ 200 (Freelance)	Lunches out	$ 30
	Rent	$ 675
	Telephone	$ 55
	Cable TV	$ 25
	Gas	$ 95
	Electricity	$ 150
	Water	$ 45
	Car payment	$ 285
	Food	$ 700
	Insurance (life and health)	$ 350
	Insurance (car)	$ 125
	Clothing	$ 75
	Emergency fund	$ 50
$2,900 (Total Income)	Total Expenses	$2,760

The couple in the budget illustrated here are saving money every month for a down payment on a house. Notice that this is *the very first entry* in their plan. Sara has $100 drafted from her salary directly into a savings account each month *before* she sees her check. That way, she and Phil are never tempted to spend the money.

You may not be able to save $100 a month, but you can save *some* amount. The important principle here is to form the habit of saving on a regular basis. To create a budget that you can live with in the present, but that also allows you to plan for the future, keep a number of key points in mind.

Always overestimate variable expenses. When you budget for expenses that fluctuate, enter the amount paid for the highest bill in that category during the past year. In my case, for example, our gas bill is higher in the winter, so I look for the month we used the most gas and enter that amount in the budget for gas. That way, I know I'll always have enough money set aside for that bill. It's money in our pocket if the bill is less one month, and it's extra insurance in case one of the other bills increases unexpectedly. Do the same thing with credit card bills. It's much more fun to find out that you have a little extra money than to discover you don't have enough to make it until the end of the month.

Set aside a certain portion of your income for those annoying, unexpected expenses that seem to happen when we are least prepared for them—like the broken furnace on the coldest day of the year, or little Jenny's falling and knocking out a tooth, or having the stalled car towed twenty miles to the repair shop. It's impossible to anticipate exactly what emergency may arise, but it is virtually certain that, at some point, one will. Plan for it. Designate an "emergency fund" category in your monthly budget, with the understanding that such money is to be used only in a genuine emergency.

Look again at Table 2.1. Although it looks as if Sara and Phil would end up with a surplus of $140 in January, they couldn't foresee that their old furnace would break down and cost $500 for repairs. Rather than rob their building fund, Sara and Phil reached an agreement with the repair shop that they would pay off the balance, using the $50 emergency fund each month.

If an emergency should arise and your funds won't cover the costs, write the creditor and let him know your payment will be delayed. Then pay the bill as soon as possible, or send a partial payment to show good faith. Try to agree with your creditor on a payment schedule that you can meet. This tactic should be your last resort and used only when absolutely necessary, however; otherwise, you will jeopardize your credit rating.

Make sure everyone in the household understands and is willing to cooperate with the budget. If the designated bookkeeper becomes unable to pay the bills for some reason, then someone else must be capable of taking over the financial situation. There should also be some basic agreement on how the money will be spent. It can be very disheartening and frustrating if one member of a family spends money unwisely while the others are trying their best to maintain a budget.

In our home, I am in charge of our finances. When my husband wants to spend money, he checks with me to see if the purchase will fit our budget. This relieves him of the money management duties and allows him to focus on the jobs that suit him better. We've seen other types of couples, though. In one household, the spouse who brings home the paycheck spends it right away, while the other individual has the impossible task of managing the vanishing money. In the other, one spouse brings home the money and tries to manage it while the other spends it. No money management system will work for long without the cooperation of all concerned. The best budget is the simplest budget that all parties can understand and agree to live by.

Revise your budget every six months or so to keep up with any new bills or other changes in your financial picture. If you have new bills, or have difficulty remembering when bills are due, put a reminder on your calendar on the date the payments are due.

Most importantly, budget money for the future. When times are tough and the money is tight, it might seem impossible to budget savings, but you can almost always put a small amount aside *if you remember to pay yourself first*. And why shouldn't you? After all, you work hard and you deserve to reward yourself.

SAVING

There are a myriad of ways to save money—from literally hiding the money in a sock under the mattress to sophisticated annuities that allow you to save and defer taxes until retirement. I am chiefly concerned here with tips for the individual who has trouble starting a savings program. I consider checking accounts here, also.

As I have already indicated, one of the very first steps in drawing up a budget should be to set aside a specific amount of each paycheck for savings. Even if it's only a dollar or so per pay period, decide on an amount that fits into your budget and try to stick with it. The savings may seem microscopic at first, but the amounts can add up over a year's time. Pay your savings "bill" first, before you pay your other debts, and before all the money has disappeared.

Choosing a Bank Account

Even if you have just a few dollars in savings, I don't recommend that you hide it around the house or bury it in the yard like a bone. First of all, as long as the money is close by, the temptation to spend it might be overwhelming. Second, there's always the chance the money might be lost or stolen. Third, as long as the savings isn't earning you any interest, it's "lazy" money that will not grow.

If you have only small amounts to save each pay period, you should open a savings account at a convenient bank or, if you are eligible to join one, a credit union. (A credit union is a financial organization of members with like interests; if the company where you work, for example, doesn't operate a credit union, you might see if other employees are interested in starting one.) If you have children, you might want to make an event out of opening an account in their names. This would be a good occasion to explain to them about the importance of saving; reinforce this by routinely taking the children with you when you make deposits. And remember, except for dire emergencies, the money you save should not be removed unless you have planned in advance to use it for a specific goal; don't use your savings account like a revolving door, with the money going in one day and out the next. Here's a

Taxes and Saving

This guide is not intended as a tax manual, and I certainly am not an expert on tax policy. However, depending on the tax bracket you are in, clearly one of the greatest impediments to saving money is the amount of taxes you pay. From time to time I will point out certain options you should be aware of; you should investigate these choices and how they might work to save you money.

One option many people use for saving money is not really a savings plan at all. By claiming fewer exemptions than they are entitled to on their W-4 forms, some people receive a big chunk of money as an income tax refund at the end of the year. These people always seem ecstatic, thinking they have somehow or another outsmarted the Internal Revenue Service. If you are tempted to use this strategy, you should understand that it amounts to allowing the government to use your money interest-free for a whole year. "Saving" this way should not be done unless this is the only way you can hold onto your money. Try to adjust your exemptions so you keep as much of your money as possible but don't have to pay any back at the end of the year. Remember, by having the money earlier, you can invest it and earn additional money, or you can use it to pay bills and avoid borrowing, thus avoiding additional interest charges. This way you save twice.

checklist of points to keep in mind when you're shopping for a place to keep your money.

Select the bank or credit union that offers the most services and the greatest return for the least amount of money. Check interest rates. Compound interest, in which the interest you receive remains in the account and you are then paid interest on the interest, can be tricky to understand. Because of compounding, the highest annual interest rate is not necessarily the best. Is interest compounded annually, semiannually, monthly, or daily? The more often the compounding, the better; daily is the best. A rate of 5 percent annually, if compounded daily, has an *effective yield* of 5.13 percent. Most banks post the effective yield, which is the true interest rate after compounding. If it's not posted, ask your banker.

Find out if an account has a service charge every month, or if there is a charge when your balance goes below a certain minimum. Many checking accounts, and some savings accounts, have a monthly service charge. With a checking account, is there a flat-rate service charge, or is there a per-check charge? Many banks now offer "free" checking accounts if you maintain a minimum balance in the account or keep a specified minimum in that bank's savings plans. Of course, if you select this option, you must tie up part of your money all the time— so it's not free after all—and you have the additional chore of making certain that your balance does not fall below the minimum, because if it does you will pay a substantial fee. Depending on your particular needs, and on how many checks you write per month, one type of account might save you several dollars a month over another.

Find out if you have to pay for transactions at automatic teller machines (ATMs). Some banks charge you for using automatic teller machines no matter which bank the ATMs belong to; other banks charge you only if you access your account through another bank's ATM. On the other hand, some banks will give you a discount off your monthly service charges for doing all of your normal teller transactions through the ATM. If a college student or another member of your family lives in an area where your bank does not have a branch, sometimes your home bank will allow free access through another bank's ATMs just to retain your business. Just ask your banker. Your lack of knowledge may be costing you extra.

Decide which type of check is best for you. Usually the least expensive is the plain check with a regular check register. Fancy designs, check stubs, and checks with carbons all cost more money. If you're extremely forgetful about entering the amount of your checks into your register, however, the carbons may be worth the extra cost for you.

Look into the possibility of ordering your checks by mail, rather than through your bank. Current, Classic Checks, and Checks in the Mail are three companies that sell checks through the mail—usually at a price that is substantially lower than the bank's. Most of these companies also offer an introductory box at even greater savings.

Ask your banker about a debit card. Recently some banks have been offering a new means of payment called a debit card. When you use a debit card to make a purchase, the amount of the purchase is electronically withdrawn from your checking or savings account and transferred to the payee. Although a debit card may look like a credit card, it is actually a different form of checking. It has several advantages, however, in that a debit card is easier to carry than a checkbook and should be more readily accepted. Unlike credit cards, debit cards normally require no annual fee, and since payment occurs at the actual time of purchase, there are no interest charges. (Just make sure that you record your debits the same way you would your checks, or you may find yourself looking at overdraft charges.)

If your employer offers it, take advantage of direct deposit of your paycheck to your bank. You will have faster access to your money with direct deposit, and you won't have to worry about whether your bank is open. Also, you can avoid those long lines on payday (if you've waited in line at the drive-thru window with your car's engine idling, you'll save the gasoline, too). Some financial institutions give discounts on loans to customers who have direct deposit.

When you're shopping around for a bank, find out how long you have to wait after a check is deposited before you can use the money. The laws governing how long a check may be held vary from state to state, and within those regulations there can be considerable differences in policy from bank to bank. Many people think their paychecks are deposited right away, only to find out—when they write other checks that bounce—that there had been a hold on the deposit.

If your bank changes hands, find out what the new policies are. One of my friends found out about policy changes the hard way. Under the old management there had been a three-day hold on checks, but the new management instituted a five-day hold on checks. She had to stop writing checks altogether because of all the accumulated charges for checks returned for insufficient funds. Besides paying deficit charges to her bank, she had to pay charges to each of her creditors' banks, too.

Check to see what your bank's policy is concerning insufficient funds. Some banks will return your check if you didn't have enough money in your account on the day the check was written. If your bank has this policy and you write the wrong date on your check, you may have to pay for that mistake.

Does your bank have overdraft protection available for your checks? Is there a charge for this? If it's a per-check charge, keep in mind that checks aren't always cashed in the order they're written. If you take the chance and write a check on insufficient funds, you may have to pay the overdraft charge on more than one check if a big check clears before the smaller ones do.

Find out what your bank's policy is on dormancy. A friend of mine ran across this problem when she made a deposit to an infrequently used checking account and then wrote a check on it. Her check was returned with a notation of insufficient funds. This confused her because she knew there was enough money in her account. What had happened was that the bank had never notified her that the account was dormant. A search had to be initiated to find her deposit and her account. To avoid this problem, find out how long your account can be inactive before it's considered dormant.

If you don't have a checking account, you may pay your bills by cashier's check or money order. If you must use a money order, make sure you purchase it through the Post Office or a federally insured financial institution. Otherwise, you might lose your money if the issuing company declares bankruptcy before the money order clears. Cashier's checks are more expensive than money orders, but they are guaranteed for sure.

Other Savings Plans

A basic savings and checking plan is not the only way of maintaining your money. In fact, many financial counselors recommend that you park only a minimum amount in a "safe" savings location, like a local bank or credit union, for liquidity (immediate, penalty-free accessibility) in case of an emergency. The remainder can be invested in various ways—like stocks, bonds, money market funds, and real estate—that offer the potential of a greater return on your money. My purpose here isn't to serve as an investment counselor, but you should be aware that, in general, the higher the return, the riskier the investment. I am concerned only with ways you might save your money on a risk-free basis, and in that direction I should mention two other savings vehicles—United States savings bonds and certificates of deposit.

Currently there are two types of U.S. savings bonds. A Series EE bond is a contract showing that you have lent a certain amount of money to the government of the United States, which promises to repay the loan along with accrued interest. Bonds are available in denominations of $50, $75, $100, and up, through $10,000. The purchase price is one-half the denomination, and the original maturity is for twelve years. Thus, a $100 EE bond costs $50 to buy, and can be redeemed in twelve years. Interest rates vary, depending on how long the bond is kept, and on market rates.

Series HH bonds are current-income securities (interest is paid semiannually and based on a fixed rate set at the time of purchase); they are issued only in exchange for Series EE or older bonds, for an original maturity of ten years. Savings bonds are tax-exempt on the state and local level, and while you still have to pay federal taxes on the interest, payment can be deferred until the bonds mature. Check with the IRS for the current tax status.

A certificate of deposit (CD) is another way to save money that is virtually risk free. Essentially, a CD is a contract between you and a financial institution that indicates how much money you will place into an account, for how long, and the rate of interest the bank or credit union will pay you for using that money. CDs are usually purchased in amounts of $1,000 or more, and the time of investment is usually six months or more. The bigger the CD, the less time is required for the investment. The bigger the CD and the longer the investment period, the higher the rate of interest for which you will be eligible. Interest rates are usually tied to economic indices based on the financial market, but they vary from bank to bank, so shop around and find the best rate before you commit your money. There usually are severe financial penalties if you need to withdraw your money before the CD has matured, so you should invest only as much as you can live without for the entire term of the CD.

U. S. savings bonds and CDs are not as liquid as basic savings plans, but they do offer an intermediate step for the individual who has more savings than he or she needs in a passbook account yet is not quite ready to plunge into the greater risk and uncertainty of the stock or bond markets. Wherever you decide to place your savings, remember, it's your money and you worked hard for it. Only invest what you can live without for the term of the investment, and shop around for the best interest rate and the fewest restrictions on you and your money.

Smart Banking

In this era of plastic and electronic banking, when access to your money seems almost too easy, you should always exercise caution to protect yourself from mistakes and criminal activity that can rob you of your money. The following are simple precautions that can help save you from becoming a victim of an error or of fraudulent activity, either of which could cost you much money and/or time.

  Write your checks in ink and make sure you fill in all the blanks. Extend a solid line to the end of the amount blank; don't leave any openings for anyone else to add anything.

  Use the memo blank on your checks to write in the account number from your bills. If your bill and check are separated, your account can be credited promptly if the creditor can find the account number on your check.

  If you're depositing checks by mail or through an ATM, write "For Deposit Only [your bank's name] Acct. # [your account number]" after your endorsement. If you want to pay someone with a check you received from someone else, endorse it and write "Pay to the Order of [name]." Anyone can deposit money into your account, but your signature is needed to take it out.

Avoid using ATMs after dark if they are not well lighted and in a conspicuous area. If you must use an ATM under adverse conditions, have another adult with you. Watch out for suspicious-looking people. If in doubt, cancel your transaction.

Don't write your personal identification number (PIN) on your ATM card. There are methods now readily available to copy the magnetic strip from your card. With a copy of your magnetic strip and your PIN, a thief can gain access to your funds even if the card is back in your possession..

When punching in your PIN, block the view of the number pad on the ATM with your body. It's better to be suspicious than to have someone lift your card and use information you "gave" them to empty your account.

CREDIT

Ideally, except in times of extreme inflation, you would be better off if you never purchased anything on credit. If you could only wait, budget, and save your money, you could pay cash for the things you want and avoid a huge surcharge through the interest you pay. Unfortunately, most people are not willing to wait. Moreover, large purchases—like automobiles or houses—would require that you save for years and years, and even then most people would not be in the financial position to pay cash.

Because of the allure of buying now and paying later, credit can lead you into a dungeon of debt so fast that it may seem like you will never escape. In fact, we are so besieged by offers of easy credit cards and "instant money" that it's no small wonder our entire nation, including the federal government, seems to be wallowing in debt. This is why I saved credit for last; for many of us, our financial success or failure will depend on how we manage our credit.

Most consumers have some kind of charge account, whether it is with a neighborhood grocer, a major credit card company like American Express, a bank card provider like Visa or MasterCard, a department store, or an oil company. Nowadays it seems like you need the ubiquitous credit card to do almost everything, from renting a videotape to installing a telephone.

However, there are major pitfalls when using credit cards; they can be dangerous to your economic health. We are often led to believe that all the wonderful things shown in the television commercials can be ours with the right card. Indeed, many times we are *persuaded* to apply for and obtain a credit card when we really don't want or need it. Then we find ourselves giving in to temptation and using this plastic money to charge up to the limit, without regard for the large payment and high interest due at the end of the month.

While credit can be useful in moderation, always remember what it really is: Credit is paying for the privilege of borrowing someone else's money. As a wise consumer who is guarding your own financial well-being, you must utilize your credit with prudence.

Establishing Credit

The best time to apply for credit is before you need it. You should establish a line of credit as soon as possible. Even though a significant number of women and young people are now working, it's often difficult to qualify for credit, so it's important to establish credit in your own name—not in the name of a parent or spouse—as soon as possible. When you marry, don't consolidate all your charge accounts with your spouse's. Maintain a good credit history in your own name in case something should happen to your spouse or in case your circumstances should change. If you should get divorced, for example, you could lose your credit cards and credit rating if you don't have credit of your own. This is especially important for women. It's easier for a husband to drop his wife's name from a credit card than it is for a wife to drop her husband's name.

If you don't have an established credit history, you might want to apply first for a credit card from a department store or oil company. These are usually easier to get than a major credit card like Visa or MasterCard. Once you have a good credit record (that is, once you have established that you can and will repay your debts on time), try applying for a major credit card.

When choosing a credit card, don't let slick advertising sell you without checking out the competition. Shop around. Note the *annual percentage rate* (APR). The lower the APR, the less you're going to be paying for your credit. Because major credit cards—like Visa and Master-Card—may be issued by a variety of financial institutions, APRs may vary significantly from one card to another. Also, make certain you understand whether the rate is fixed or floating. Floating rates can change from month to month, and what is a relatively low APR when you select the card may creep up later.

Frequently the interest rate is quoted as a monthly rate, such as 1.5 percent, which can be confusing. To find the APR, simply multiply the monthly rate by 12. For example, a monthly rate of 1.5 percent, which doesn't sound too intimidating, actually works out to be an APR of 18 percent, which is much higher than the normal interest rate on a personal loan.

In addition to interest rates, find out whether there is an annual cardholder's fee and how much it is. An annual fee is charged in addition to the APR, and you may receive an unexpected surprise once a year when the fee is billed to your account. Some card accounts require an additional annual fee if you have more than one cardholder; other accounts maintain the same fee no matter how many cards are issued. If you have several cards with annual fees of fifty dollars or so, you could be paying a lot of extra money for your credit, so keep the number of cards with fees to one or, at most, two. With today's competitive market, you should be able to secure a card with no annual fee, but remember to check the fine print for "hidden" charges, which might outweigh the savings.

Hidden costs might include a set late fee that is independent of the amount of your purchase. In other words, the late fee might be fifteen dollars—regardless of whether your purchase was five dollars or seventy-five dollars. This fee is in addition to the interest you pay, of course. Another charge you may not notice unless you read carefully can result from the lack of a "grace period." The time from the day of your purchase to the date payment is due is known as the grace period. Many cards do not begin charging interest on the amount of a purchase until the due date. Other cards, however, begin assessing interest charges from the day of your purchase. Thus, without a grace period, you will always pay more than the original purchase price, even if you pay off your credit card balance by the due date. Also, remember that most credit cards have different payment schedules for cash advances, which are usually more expensive than regular purchases.

Finally, be wary of incentive programs. Many credit cards offer incentives, like a 1-percent rebate, or insurance for products, when their customers make purchases. Compare the APRs of various credit cards to find out if the card with the incentives will charge you higher interest for these benefits.

Using Your Credit Cards

Now that you have applied for and received one or more credit cards, the real fun will begin. Now you will have an opportunity to demonstrate that self-control you're so proud of—and, if you're like most Americans, you'll need every ounce of discipline you can muster. Just remember, *your goal is to use credit to assist you in managing your money.* Here are a few tips to keep in mind.

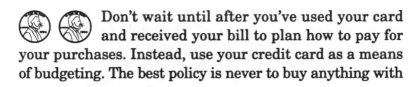 Be aware of your credit limit. It may shrink or expand depending on how you use your card and how successful you are at paying off your debt. If you don't use your credit card often, your limit may shrink, but it can be expanded if you need more credit and have proved you can pay your bills on time.

Don't wait until after you've used your card and received your bill to plan how to pay for your purchases. Instead, use your credit card as a means of budgeting. The best policy is never to buy anything with your credit card that you can't pay off at the end of the billing period. If you make sure to choose a card that gives you a grace period, as long as you pay the total amount billed you never pay a finance charge. In essence, you receive an interest-free loan for the days during the billing cycle. In addition, the card company or bank provides you with free written statements for your records each month. Remember, interest on credit cards and revolving charge accounts is no longer tax deductible, so *there is absolutely no advantage in paying high interest rates!*

Make your monthly payments as large as your budget will allow. Of course, it is difficult always to have the money to pay off the total amount billed every month, but this should be your goal. Although different credit card companies calculate your interest and payments differently, inevitably the interest will be compounded rather than simple, meaning you end up paying interest on the interest—as well as on the principal.

For example, let's say you need a new refrigerator and freezer but don't have the cash right now. You decide to charge the $1,000 purchase to your credit card, which charges 1.5 percent interest a month; and since your budget is always tight, you decide to make only the 5-percent minimum monthly payment required until the debt is cleared. With this minimum payment, after eighty-four months—or seven years—you will still owe a balance of $46.98, and you will have paid close to $400 in interest for borrowing the original $1,000. This is an extreme example to prove a point, of course, because making only the 5-percent minimum payment each month means you take a long time to pay off the purchase; the larger your payments and the sooner you pay down the balance, the less interest you will pay. Nevertheless, many people do get caught up in a vicious cycle of charging so much to their credit cards that they can afford to make only minimum payments. If this happens to you, take action immediately to end your reliance on credit.

Use any extra money you have to pay off your bills. If you have just a little extra money, it may not make any difference which bill you choose to pay. If it's a bigger chunk of money, apply it where it will do the most good. You may be able to eliminate a bill entirely. Notice how your payments are computed on each account. With some credit cards, if you make a larger payment, it will lower the amount of subsequent required monthly payments. Other credit card companies count a larger payment only toward the next payment due, so that your bills will state "no payment due at this time" until your advance payment catches up with their billing schedule. Send in at least the minimum payment even if there's "no payment due at this time." This will reduce your interest charges, and you'll be ahead in your payments if an emergency comes up and you don't have enough money to pay that bill for one month.

Know the closing dates of your credit card bills and use them to your advantage. For example, if your Visa card closes on the tenth of the month, and your MasterCard closes on the twenty-fifth, a purchase on the fifth of the month should be charged to the Master-Card. If you charge it on the Visa, payment for your purchase will come due within thirty-five days—five days to the closing date plus the thirty-day grace period. On the MasterCard, however, payment will not come due for fifty days—twenty days until the closing plus the thirty-day grace period. Obviously, this option allows your money to remain in the bank longer, earning interest for you. Similarly, a purchase you make on the twentieth of the month should be charged to your Visa card.

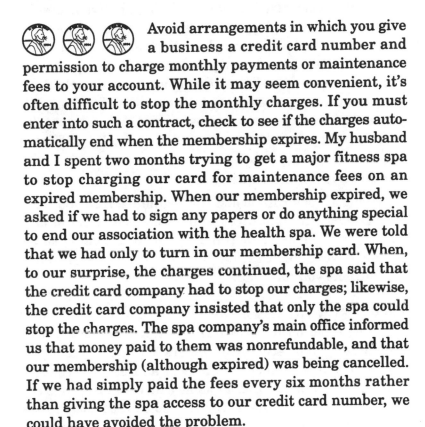 Avoid arrangements in which you give a business a credit card number and permission to charge monthly payments or maintenance fees to your account. While it may seem convenient, it's often difficult to stop the monthly charges. If you must enter into such a contract, check to see if the charges automatically end when the membership expires. My husband and I spent two months trying to get a major fitness spa to stop charging our card for maintenance fees on an expired membership. When our membership expired, we asked if we had to sign any papers or do anything special to end our association with the health spa. We were told that we had only to turn in our membership card. When, to our surprise, the charges continued, the spa said that the credit card company had to stop our charges; likewise, the credit card company insisted that only the spa could stop the charges. The spa company's main office informed us that money paid to them was nonrefundable, and that our membership (although expired) was being cancelled. If we had simply paid the fees every six months rather than giving the spa access to our credit card number, we could have avoided the problem.

Be extremely cautious of advertisements that promise deferred payment on purchases for several months or "until next year." These offers sound terrific, but you should first check to see how much down payment is necessary and then ask if interest will accumulate during the period that payments are deferred. Otherwise, you might be shocked to discover how much you actually owe when "next year" comes around.

  Consider layaway as an alternative to credit. Although it is not as common as it once was, some stores still offer this plan. Ask! With layaway, you choose the item you plan to purchase and give the store a down payment—usually a nominal amount—to hold it for you. You then pay the balance over a three- to six-month period. There is little or no interest charged because you take possession of your purchase only when it is fully paid for.

Protecting Your Credit

Receiving a credit card is just the beginning. Now you have to take measures to protect your cards, just as you would cash. To avoid being a victim of credit card criminals and to protect your credit rating, here are some commonsense precautions you can take.

  Write down the numbers of each of your accounts and put the list in a safe place. Memorizing your account numbers is even better if you can do it. Put the phone numbers or addresses to contact in case of theft or loss in that same safe place. If your credit cards are lost or stolen, you'll need to report the missing cards promptly; cardholders can be held liable for some charges (usually the first fifty dollars) if the theft is not reported immediately, even if the card is used fraudulently.

  Mutilate (cut up) expired or unwanted cards so they'll be unreadable. Thieves spend hours sorting through trash searching for old credit cards. Sign your new cards immediately, and *don't* walk around with an unsigned card in your purse or wallet. Your signature on the card, which can be matched with your signature on a receipt when you make a purchase, proves that it's *your* card. If another individual gets an opportunity to sign the card, it is much easier for him to use it because when he signs the purchase slip, he is simply matching his own handwriting.

Give your card number over the phone *only* when you've initiated the call and know the reputation of the recipient, and *never* when using a cellular or portable telephone. Ordering merchandise over the phone is very convenient, but don't order anything unless you're the one who makes the call. Be very careful about providing *any* confidential information unnecessarily unless you know the person you're speaking to. Account numbers, such as for credit or utilities, and social security numbers make nice little toeholds for a prospective thief. My husband once talked to someone on a computer bulletin board who claimed that he could eradicate our bills electronically. My husband promptly hung up because he wasn't interested in anything illegal. Later, we realized that with our account numbers, an electronic thief could have charged all kinds of purchases to our accounts.

Don't write your account number on a postcard offer unless you intend to send the postcard in an envelope. The envelope may cost a few extra cents in postage, but you'll prevent unauthorized access to your account number. I recommend that you never write account numbers on the outsides of envelopes. If you must, put outgoing mail directly into a government mailbox rather than leaving it for the mail carrier to pick up. The mail carrier may be trustworthy, but someone else could appropriate one of your bills and use your account number.

If you receive mail that says you qualify for a specified credit card and you aren't going to apply, destroy the form so that no one else can use the form in your name.

Keep an eye on your card when it's in someone else's possession—while in the hands of a salesperson or clerk, for example. The card could be misplaced or used unscrupulously to create a second receipt. Make sure you sign only one receipt per transaction. Two receipts can easily be imprinted with your card number, and you could sign them both without noticing. When you sign a second receipt, you're giving dishonest people a blank check to use any way they wish.

If a credit form uses separate carbons, remember to ask for them. Rip the carbons into bits so they can't be pieced together. It's possible for someone to obtain your account number from the carbon and use it without your signature.

Don't carry extra credit cards around with you. The fewer cards you carry, the less risk there is of loss or theft. I recommend that you have only one or two cards that can be used in a variety of places.

Keep your receipts and compare them to your monthly statements. If there are discrepancies, report them immediately. It takes awhile to straighten out billing errors, and the longer you wait to report any problems, the longer you'll be paying interest on the incorrect amount.

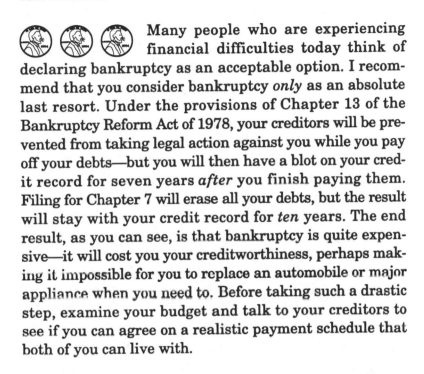 Many people who are experiencing financial difficulties today think of declaring bankruptcy as an acceptable option. I recommend that you consider bankruptcy *only* as an absolute last resort. Under the provisions of Chapter 13 of the Bankruptcy Reform Act of 1978, your creditors will be prevented from taking legal action against you while you pay off your debts—but you will then have a blot on your credit record for seven years *after* you finish paying them. Filing for Chapter 7 will erase all your debts, but the result will stay with your credit record for *ten* years. The end result, as you can see, is that bankruptcy is quite expensive—it will cost you your creditworthiness, perhaps making it impossible for you to replace an automobile or major appliance when you need to. Before taking such a drastic step, examine your budget and talk to your creditors to see if you can agree on a realistic payment schedule that both of you can live with.

Loans

Credit cards are not the only form of credit; they merely represent a way of obtaining instant loans, and for the convenience and speed of credit cards you usually pay a high interest rate. In many cases you would actually be much better off to examine your financial circumstances, plan your budget, and—in cases in which you absolutely must have more cash—apply for a personal loan from a bank, credit union, or other lending institution.

There are several advantages to securing a loan this way. First, your credit history will be thoroughly investigated, so you must qualify according to the lending institution's regulations. This in itself can serve as a check on those of us who cannot control our spending. Second, if you qualify, you can receive a preferred simple interest loan. This means that you pay interest on the principal only, and not on the accrued interest, and it can save you a substantial amount of money. For the most part, however, simple interest loans are available only to a bank's best customers—which means, essentially, that you have to prove you don't need the money in order to secure a loan. There are other types of loans, however.

Installment loans allow you some flexibility in selecting both the amount of your regular payments and the number of installments you make. For example, your income probably limits the amount you can afford to pay each month. By contracting for a four-year loan rather than a three-year loan, you would reduce the dollar amount of each payment by increasing the number of installments. Of course, the longer you take to pay back the loan, the more interest you must forfeit. In most cases, an installment loan takes the form of a conditional sales contract; the legal title to the item purchased is retained by the lender until you successfully complete your payments. Then the title passes over to you.

In urgent situations, you might have to consider a finance company as a potential source of credit. Finance companies often provide loans to people who cannot secure credit elsewhere. Because of the risky nature of their business, they are permitted to charge higher interest rates (often double or triple what a bank might charge). If you are forced to consider this option, beware of offers of extra-low monthly payments. If the terms seem too good to be true, examine the contract carefully. Hidden in the small print may be a penalty for paying off the loan early. Low monthly payments can also indicate a big down payment or a balloon payment—a large amount that must be paid upon completion of the contract.

If you have hidden assets in insurance or property, you would do better to explore ways to turn them into cash. If you have considerable cash reserves built up in a whole life insurance policy, for example, it can provide the cash you need at an interest rate that is usually lower than the market rates. Essentially, you can "borrow" your own money. (You can choose not to pay it back, too, but if you do you will be reducing the amount of insurance in force.) If you own or are buying a home, check out a home equity loan. Because of rising property values, your home may be worth considerably more than the amount you owe on your mortgage. This value, or *equity*, is the greatest financial asset most Americans have, yet until recently it could not be utilized until the home was sold. A home equity loan is like a second mortgage that allows you to borrow against this value, and the interest you pay is tax-deductible.

For example, let's say you purchased your home ten years ago for $30,000. You took out a thirty-year mortgage for $25,000 and still owe $23,000. Your home is now valued at $85,000, however, so you have approximately $62,000 in equity—part of which you could turn into cash by means of a home equity loan. Although the home equity loan can be an excellent source of money, usually with a good interest rate—and with the added advantage that the interest is fully tax-deductible—I caution you to be very careful not to overextend your means to repay. Since the home equity loan is based on a second mortgage on your home, if you fail to meet the payment schedule, you could lose your home.

Leasing

Many people find it difficult to come up with the large down payments frequently required to purchase a home, automobile, furniture, appliances, and other major items. Others don't want the responsibility for maintaining or moving and storing their possessions. Increasingly, many people are turning to leasing as an alternative. Leasing is simply another form of credit, in which you sign a contract to borrow whatever the product may be. In return, you pay a monthly or weekly amount for a designated period of time; then you usually have the option of purchasing the item or of turning it back over to the lessor. As with credit cards, you pay dearly for the convenience. While each individual case is different, leasing—which is just another term for renting—leaves you with no equity or asset when the contract ends, and in most instances is not recommended.

TAKING CHARGE

Are you tired of never having the money to meet your financial obligations, much less having a life raft in reserve to keep you afloat in emergencies? The very first step to economic survival is to realize that it's not good enough simply to drift from day to day, and week to week, in a sea of unpaid bills and uncontrolled expenses. It's time you took charge of your financial situation instead of allowing it to control you.

No matter what your current income level, and no matter what your present financial circumstances, you *can* determine your own financial fate. You don't have to wait for a raise or a better job, nor do you have to go back to school or pay a financial consultant. First, examine your goals and decide what you want out of life. Then you *must* plan a budget to manage your money. Based on your income, determine how much you can spend, how much you can save for the future, and—if necessary—how much credit you must have in order to survive. Only after you have such a plan can you apply it to specific goals and then measure your success. Soon, you will discover that pinching pennies can work for you just as it has for me.

3

Reducing Your Grocery Bill

Whether you live alone, with someone else, or as part of a large family, your grocery bill takes a major chunk of your income, so learning how to shop wisely is very important. Some people just go to the store and pick up whatever looks good. These people usually have higher grocery bills than the smart shoppers, who know exactly what they need and can find it quickly. Learning to shop wisely may take some extra time at first, but with practice you will save both time and money. You might even enjoy the challenge.

PLAN AHEAD

Just as you need a financial plan, or budget, if you hope to succeed in managing your money, you need a plan to manage your grocery expenses. In this case, the shopping list is your plan, and the basis for that list is your menu. Menus can be planned for the week, the month, or simply the time between shopping trips. Try to follow your menus as closely as possible, but don't be afraid to make substitutions or to vary the plan. If you have fish on your menu for Thursday, for example, but discover on your Tuesday shopping expedition that flounder is on special because it is about to pass its peak fresh date, don't hesitate to serve baked flounder in lemon sauce on Tuesday night. The menu is meant to be a help, not a straitjacket. Be flexible. The following hints will help you use planning to control the amount of money you spend on food (although paper and cleaning products are frequently purchased at grocery stores, I am concerned in this chapter only with foods; for hints on how to save on cleaning products, see Chapter 5, Home Economics).

Reduce the number of shopping trips you make. Every time you walk into a store, you will be tempted to spend money. You usually leave a store with a purchase, don't you? Think about the way stores are set up—you almost have to go through a checkout to leave the store. So if you don't find what you went in for, you may pick up something else and buy it—"as long as I'm here."

Look for sales *before* you go shopping. Check the newspaper ads for the stores you usually patronize to see if the items on your grocery list are on sale this week. You might find a better buy on many of your listed items at another store that is just as convenient. Mentally categorize the stores in your shopping range. Know which stores carry what items and the specialties of each. Which stores have double coupon offers? Do certain items tend to be on sale in certain stores? Is there a pattern to the sales on these items?

Choose the right store for your needs. There is a bigger variety and selection of stores available today than ever before. There are supermarkets, warehouses, specialty stores, convenience stores, and thrift shops. Supermarkets are the most popular because you can buy everything, even nongrocery items, in one place.

Warehouses may carry an even larger product mix, including appliances, hardware, electronic equipment, and more, as well as groceries. A common misconception is that warehouses deal only in oversized products, which is not always the case. Some warehouses do charge an annual membership fee, however, so you should make sure your savings are likely to offset the membership fee. Specialty stores—like bakeries, dairies, butcher shops, and produce stands—specialize in one type of product and are often more expensive. Convenience stores are usually the most expensive of all because they charge for the convenience of longer hours; most are small and carry only the items that are the most in demand. Thrift stores carry items that are discontinued, whose packaging has changed, or that are not considered "fresh." In a bakery thrift store, for instance, the baked goods may have passed the "fresh if sold by" date on the package. That doesn't mean they are stale, however. Although some people will not purchase day-old bread, if you stop to think about it, unless you buy your bread daily and eat it all that same day, you'll always be eating bread that is at least a day old.

  Clip coupons and keep them organized. It is usually helpful to keep coupons for similar products together, so that you can quickly find and refer to them when you're in the grocery store. Remember, a national brand purchased with a coupon may still cost more than a house brand; having your coupons organized will allow you to compare prices easily as you shop (see Coupons and Refunds, page 48).

Plan your shopping trips for times when you're not thirsty or hungry. When you're hungry,

Coupons and Refunds

Many manufacturers encourage consumers to try new products or to continue to purchase old favorites by giving us incentives in the forms of coupons and refunds. Since the costs of advertising through coupons and refunds are already added into the price of the products we purchase, if you do not take advantage of these marketing incentives, you are, in effect, paying extra. It is the consumer's job to clip and keep track of these incentives, which takes time and organizational skill, but can be well worth the effort.

You can find coupons in newspapers, in magazines, on pads in stores, and sometimes on the products themselves. A new gadget appearing in stores is the instant coupon dispenser, usually located right in front of the products the manufacturer is promoting. Some stores give out coupons printed on the back of their cash register tapes. Coupon exchanges, in which you drop in coupons you don't use and pick up ones you do use, are another source. I have seen coupon exchanges set up in grocery stores, libraries, and even churches. Of course, the simplest form of coupon exchange is to trade with your friends and neighbors.

Another source is companies such as Carol Wright, Money Mailer, and Val-U-Pak, which mail out packets of coupons for discounts on a variety of products and services. Some companies specialize in national brands; others work with local mer-

chants. Be alert for mail-in survey and request forms that can get your name on mailing lists to receive these offerings. They can often be found among the offers in your newspaper's weekly coupon insert.

Keep your eyes open for coupons on new items. Some companies offer a free trial size or the equivalent amount off a full-sized product. When new products appear in the stores, they are often sold for a special introductory price. By using coupons in combination with an introductory sale, you can save a lot of money.

In some areas, you may be able to find double- or triple-coupon days. Instead of reducing the price of the product by the face value of the coupon, the cashier takes two or three times that amount off your bill. There may be restrictions for certain products such as liquor, tobacco, or dairy products, and many stores limit the maximum amount per coupon to one dollar, or not more than the value of the item purchased. Even so, double or triple coupons can easily mean saving ten dollars or more on a single visit to the store. And remember, coupons are really a form of non-taxable income.

Don't, however, let your shopping habits be totally controlled by the available coupons, and don't succumb to the temptation to purchase an item without judging it by other criteria. Many times a house brand without a coupon will still be a better buy than a national brand with a coupon, and just because you have that terrific coupon for dog food, that doesn't mean your cat is going to eat Woofies. From the manufacturer's perspective, coupons are to stimulate buying; from your point of view, coupons should be used only when they fit into your plan to save money.

Refunds have been around since the days of Orphan Annie Ovaltine shake-up mugs and secret decoder rings. They come in the form of money, free products, toys, clothes, coupons, recipe booklets, and a host of other incentives. Each has specific directions that must be followed, and usually you must provide a proof of purchase: a seal on the package, a tear strip on a juice can, a net-weight statement, or a special marking or picture from the package. Before you send in for a refund, decide if it's worthwhile. Do you have to pay something to receive a product, or is your cost just a postage-and-handling charge? Is it worth even that small charge? Do you buy the product often?

In addition to coupons and refunds, there are rain checks that can help you save money. If a store advertises that a certain item is on sale, they are supposed to have enough stock on hand to meet the demand (unless the ad specifically notes that only limited quantites are available). If they run out of an advertised sale item, you can usually get a rain check, which enables you to buy the item at the sale price once it is in stock again. Like coupons, rain checks usually have expiration dates, so you should redeem them as soon as possible. Most stores will give you a rain check—but you have to ask for one; they are not required to offer it. For the greatest savings, try to combine coupons, refunds, rain checks, and sale prices for the products you purchase.

even an old tire looks good enough to eat, and the urge to buy on impulse is very strong. Food looks less appealing on a full stomach, making it far easier to stick to your shopping list.

SHOP WISELY

Think of shopping as a friendly battle of wits between large corporations, with tremendous financial resources at their disposal, and individuals like you and me. (Of course, there are still some smaller, owner-operated stores around, but even then it's probably a useful image.) On their side, they have the power of advertising, packaging, and many other subtle tactics to manipulate you into spending your dollars. They also have on their side the undeniable biological fact that you must buy food in order to live; it's just a matter of where you will buy it and how much you will spend.

On the other hand, your only weapon is your own individual skill: You must know what you need and plan to achieve your goal without regard to the distractions set out to tempt you. You must be prepared to go on the offensive, to plan your strategy and take decisive action. Everything in a modern grocery store is placed by design (usually after extensive marketing studies) to increase the chances that it will be sold quickly and at a good profit. In order to do your best at *your* job, you need to be alert and follow a plan. Consider the following guidelines.

Avoid crowded stores. Large crowds may break your concentration and encourage you to pick up the first thing you see to remove yourself from the path of other shoppers; it's very difficult to focus on saving a few pennies on a jar of peanut butter when you're in danger of being run down by a speeding grocery cart. Try to find out which days the stores are less crowded. For example, Fridays, Saturdays, and the fifteenth and thirtieth of the month are usually crowded days, so you'd probably want to avoid doing your shopping then. Shopping early in the morning or later at night helps you avoid crowds, keeps you out of long lines, and can help you save money on your grocery bill. Standing in a long checkout line not only wastes your time, it also increases the chances that you will be tempted by all the products on the ends of the aisles and near the checkout.

If at all possible, leave the kids at home with a friend or other family member. You obviously can't concentrate on prices while rescuing little Jimmy from the coffee grinder or restraining baby Ashley from climbing that mountain of canned fruit.

Instead of grabbing the box of cereal or cookies that's right in front of your eyes, look around and compare prices. The placement of packages in stores is very well planned. Usually the more expensive products are on the shelves at eye level for the consumer for whom they are targeted. Most people don't like to reach or bend and will develop tunnel vision at their eye level.

Be aware of packaging, which is carefully designed to influence your decisions. Companies spend a lot of money finding out what colors will make different products appeal to you. For instance, laundry detergent packaged in green or blue boxes can suggest cleaner or fresher clothes; orange or yellow cartons can suggest brighter clothes; red or purple boxes probably would have negative connotations for most people. Generic products, with their plain labels, can be just as good as the ones in the pretty packaging.

When you are considering buying a new food product, read the package carefully to find out exactly what it contains. Not all of the food in the picture may actually be included. Read the ingredient list to make sure it's really worth the money (and to save yourself from having to make another trip to the store for the missing ingredients).

Learn to use marketing strategies to *your* advantage. Placement and packaging aren't the only influences at work in the store. Depending on the store and what is perceived as its customer base, there may be subtle, soothing music to make you more receptive to the powers of suggestion. In these stores, a soothing voice will periodically inform you of special buys or terms. Other stores will play faster, upbeat music, and in these a loud voice might announce "blue-light specials" with fanfare and urgency—like you simply *must* take advantage of the deal immediately. Indeed, sometimes you *can* save money by taking advantage of "on-the-spot" sales information, especially if you had planned to purchase the product anyhow. In most cases, however, you would be better off to ignore the store's siren song to spend more money and stick to your list.

Try to buy in season. Most fruits and vegetables have a season when they are more plentiful and therefore less expensive. Since not all types of produce have the same season, you should learn as much

as you can about the various types and buy accordingly
(see Fresh Produce Seasons and Storage, page 56). Learn
how produce should look and feel; make sure it's ripe yet
not on the verge of spoiling. Ask the produce manager for
help if you're not sure. Take pride in educating yourself
about what to purchase, and soon others will be coming to
you for help.

Understand the difference between name
brands, house brands, and generics. National
name brands have national advertising, distribute coupons
widely, and are sold in many different stores. A house or
store brand is manufactured for and carried by a particular chain of stores. If there are any coupons available for
a house brand, they are usually distributed by that chain.
In some cases there is little or no difference between the
ingredients in the name brand and those in a house brand
because both are produced by the same company. Generic
products usually cost the least of all because there is little or no advertising, no coupons, and nondescript labels.
Compare both price and quality among the different brands
to find the best buy for you. If you've tried the generic
brand and your family will eat only Brand X, Brand X may
be the better buy even though it is more expensive.

Buy in quantities you can use. You may not need a
gallon jar of mayonnaise or that huge head of cab-
bage. You should buy your food according to how much you
will eat, how soon you will eat it, and how you will store
it. Of course, this is especially true for perishable items
like fresh fruit and vegetables, meats, and bread. The shelf
life of many items, even when refrigerated, is quite brief.
Here again, you must educate yourself on the optimum

storage time for your perishables and determine whether each should be placed in the pantry, refrigerator, or freezer. Don't buy the large economy size unless you will be able to use or save it all, even if it does cost considerably less per pound.

Always check for unit pricing—the price per pound, ounce, or serving—which is usually displayed on the shelf. Many times we are led to believe that the large economy size is automatically a better buy than the smaller sizes. But this is not always true; the bigger size may not always be the bargain. Unit pricing is also important if two similar items are displayed together: one may show the total cost for the product while the other shows the price per pound. Take a minute to calculate the better buy. (If you haven't formed the habit of carrying a pocket calculator *everywhere* you shop, now is the time to begin.)

Reduce your dependence on convenience foods. These products received their name because much of the work to prepare them has been done by someone else. Thus, you are paying not only for the food, but for preparation and packaging as well. Admittedly, in this fast-paced, hard-working world of ours, it is frequently difficult to find the time to cook meals from scratch. However, in most cases, *if you plan ahead of time*, you and your family can find ways to create imaginative, economical meals. Since many convenience foods are notoriously high in saturated fat, sodium, sugar, and many other unhealthy additives, you will have the additional bonus of improving the nutritional value of your food, perhaps even having a positive effect on the health of everyone concerned. One simple trick is to make a double recipe of whatever meal you

Table 3.1 Fresh Produce Seasons and Storage

Vegetable	Peak Season*	Storage Recommendations
Asparagus	April–June	Wrap in damp cloth or waxed paper and store in the refrigerator.
Beans, green/wax	March–August	Store in plastic in the refrigerator for up to several days.
Beans, lima	July–November	Store in the refrigerator at high humidity. Shell just before cooking.
Beets	June–October	Store in the refrigerator (up to three weeks) or in a root cellar (several months).
Broccoli	October–March	Store in plastic in the refrigerator at high humidity for up to one week.
Brussels sprouts	November–January	Store in the refrigerator at high humidity for up to one week.
Cabbage	October–March	Store in a root cellar or in the refrigerator at high humidity. Do not cut until ready to use.
Carrots	All year	Store in plastic in the refrigerator at high humidity, or in a root cellar.
Cauliflower	October–December	Store in the refrigerator at high humidity.
Celery	November–May	Wrap in plastic and store in the refrigerator.
Corn, sweet	May–October	Best eaten right away, not stored, but if you must, keep very cold and at high humidity. Remove the husks only when ready to cook.
Cucumbers	May–August	Store in the refrigerator at average humidity.
Eggplant	July–September	Wrap and store in the refrigerator for up to several days.

* Seasons for locally grown produce may vary slightly, depending on geographical location.

Vegetable	Peak Season	Storage Recommendations
Lettuce	May–July	Store in the refrigerator. Iceberg must be kept completely dry in a sealed container; other types may be washed and shaken dry before storage.
Mushrooms	November–December	Store in a brown paper bag in the refrigerator for up to four or five days. Clean only before using, and do not wash with water; use a vegetable brush instead.
Onions	All year	Keep in a cool, dry, well-ventilated place (but preferably not the refrigerator).
Parsley	October–December	Store wrapped in plastic in the refrigerator for up to approximately three weeks.
Peas	May–August	Best eaten right away, but can be stored in the refrigerator for several days if necessary. Shell just before cooking.
Peppers, sweet	Summer	Store in the refrigerator at average humidity for up to one week.
Potatoes	All year	Store in a dry, dark, well-ventilated, and cool area (for several weeks) or in a root cellar (for four to six months). Do not store in the refrigerator or expose to light.
Radishes	Late spring	Store in the refrigerator for up to one week.
Scallions	All year	Store in the refrigerator. If the tops dry out, cut them off and use the rest.
Spinach	April–May	Store in plastic in the refrigerator.
Squash, winter	October–December	Store in any room that is not hot or humid.
Squash, summer	May–August	Store in the refrigerator for up to one week.

Vegetable	Peak Season	Storage Recommendations
Sweet potatoes	All year	Store in a cool place or in a root cellar.
Turnips	October–November	Store in the refrigerator (for one week) or in a root cellar (for longer periods of time).

Fruit	Peak Season	Storage Recommendations
Apples	June–November	Store in the refrigerator for up to several weeks or in a root cellar.
Apricots	June–September	Best eaten as soon as they ripen, but can be stored in the refrigerator if necessary.
Avocados	January–May	Store at room temperature, and do not cut until ripe. After cutting, wrap unused fruit tightly and store in the refrigerator.
Bananas	All year	Allow to ripen at room temperature until skins are flecked with brown. Ripe bananas can be stored in the refrigerator for several days (the skins will turn brown, but the fruit will remain fresh).
Blueberries	May–August	Store in the refrigerator for up to several days. Can also be frozen in an airtight container.
Cantaloupe	May–September	Allow to ripen at room temperature. Best eaten as soon as they ripen, but ripe melons can be stored in the refrigerator for a few days if necessary.
Cherries	June–July	Store in the refrigerator, and eat as soon as possible.
Cranberries	October–December	Store in the refrigerator for four to eight weeks, or in the freezer for longer periods. Keep them dry.

Fruit	Peak Season	Storage Recommendations
Grapes	August–November	Best eaten as soon as possible, but can be stored in the refrigerator for up to two weeks if necessary.
Grapefruit	January–May	Store in the refrigerator. Do not cut until ready to eat.
Lemons	January–May	Store in the refrigerator. Cut only before using.
Limes	All year	Store in a cool, dry place.
Nectarines	March–September	Best eaten as soon as they ripen, but can be stored in the refrigerator for a few days if necessary.
Oranges	January–May	Store in the refrigerator. Do not cut until ready to use.
Peaches	July–August	Ripe peaches can be stored in the refrigerator for one to two weeks.
Pineapples	All year	Store ripe pineapple in plastic in the refrigerator for three to five days.
Pears	Depends on variety	Ripen at room temperature or in the refrigerator. Ripe pears can be stored in the refrigerator for several days if necessary.
Plums	May–August	Ripe plums can be stored in the refrigerator for several days.
Raspberries	May–August	Best eaten right away but can be stored in the refrigerator briefly if kept dry.
Strawberries	May–June	Keep well aired out and cool, and eat as soon as possible. Can also be frozen for longer storage.
Watermelon	June–August	Ripe watermelon can be stored in the refrigerator for up to one week.

cook and freeze the second batch for a convenient meal at a later date.

Buy versatile items and plan to use leftovers efficiently. Some foods have limited uses, while others are more versatile. Take, for instance, a can of chili and a can of pinto beans. The chili, no matter what you do with it, will taste something like chili. The can of beans, on the other hand, can be used in chili, in a salad, as a side dish, or in a casserole.

Reduce your purchases of snack and dessert products. Most of these are "empty calories"— highly processed foods with lots of salt and sugar but little nutritional value. When you feel you must have a snack or dessert, try making it from scratch. Look at the ready-made snacks on the store shelves. If you know how to cook, you can probably recreate them in your kitchen for less money. An alternative to sugar-laden treats is popcorn, which you can make in minutes on top of the stove; one jar of popcorn kernels will make many batches, even though it costs about the same as a single bag of potato chips. Also, many people spend a great deal of money on dessert items simply because they have been trained to expect something sweet after every meal. You can retrain your taste buds, and in time you won't even think about eating sweets after meals.

Consider purchasing packages that are crushed, dented, stained, or cut. These items are usually placed on a special shelf; they may be tucked away in the back or a corner of the store. Examine the damaged package carefully to determine whether any seals have been broken, if there are any leaks, and whether the contents could have been contaminated by another person or insects. Boxes with cuts are usually damaged during the shelf-stocking process. They usually have an inner liner that is intact, but if they don't, the box could be taped shut with a stamp on it that says "Vet Inspected" to show that it was damaged in unpacking and there was no contamination. If you buy damaged packages, you should use them quickly

Caution: *Do not* buy cans or jars that have rounded tops or raised seals. If the top is not flat, the contents may have been contaminated by the deadly toxin that causes botulism. Even a small amount of the botulin toxin can be fatal, and it is not easily destroyed by normal cooking procedures.

Watch for dated bargains. Many stores mark down food that is close to its "sell by" date. You can often save 25 percent or more on meat and dairy items by watching for these bargains. Either use such meat the day you purchase it or put it in the freezer right away for future use. Dairy items should be used as soon as possible.

Look for sales on fruit and vegetables that are bruised or past their peak condition. Again, planning is the key to taking advantage of the lower prices available on ripe fruit and vegetables; you must know in advance that such produce will be eaten as soon as possible after purchase, or take the time to process it. When you bake fruit, for example, its original texture makes no difference in the finished product: overripe bananas can be used in banana bread, and ripe apples can be used in applesauce, pies, or strudel. Similarly, minor bruises and defects can be cut from most fruit and vegetables without affecting their edibility.

With meat, the more it is processed or cut up, the higher the price per pound. Sometimes you are lucky enough to find a store where you can buy a larger cut of meat and have a butcher cut it up for you at no extra charge. Otherwise you can do this yourself. By buying whole chickens and cutting them up you can save at least 20 percent of the cost of buying chicken that is already cut up.

At the checkout, place your big packages up against the dividers that separate your order from those of other customers. It's very easy for a small can or jar to slip around the edge of a divider. Then another customer gets charged for your item and has to return it, while you have to make another trip to the store to replace it.

Watch as your purchases and coupons are rung up. The price on the package may not be the sale price, and it is up to you to confirm that the cashier rings up the correct price. If you punched the price of each item into your calculator as you placed the item in your cart, you should know precisely what your subtotal (before taxes and coupons) is; any significant variation from your calculated total should be politely questioned. Even if you forgot your calculator, you should keep a mental note of approximately how much your total is. If your store has scanners, be very watchful; several studies have reported that scanners frequently charge an incorrect price.

Find out if the store you shop in will give you credit for reusing grocery bags, or using your own bags. More and more supermarkets, in an effort to keep their costs down, are encouraging their customers to use both plastic and paper bags for more than one shopping trip. This "bag credit" may be several cents per bag; as with coupons, this may not seem like much by itself, but it all adds up over time.

GET YOUR MONEY'S WORTH

A recent study conducted by people who study garbage concluded that Americans waste about 15 percent of the food they buy. Think about it. If your family spends $500 a month on groceries, and you are typical, you are throwing away $75 a month—or *$900* a year! You may as well throw the money in the trash and save the time and energy expended in shopping and hauling the soon-to-be-wasted groceries home!

There are many ways to cut down on waste. Shopping wisely is only part of the battle; not throwing out good food and learning how to make food go further pose even greater challenges.

Waste Not

A lot of food waste occurs before our meals even get to the table. Using food efficiently begins the moment you come home from the grocery store. Here again, you should know how and when you plan to use each item, and keep this plan in mind as you store, prepare, cook, and serve your food. To minimize waste, keep in mind the following points.

Clean and prepare foods efficiently. In restaurants, where every piece of food might make the difference between being profitable and losing money, preparers take off only the bad parts of fruits and vegetables. If the edge of a lettuce leaf is wilted, a professional food preparer will discard only the wilted part, not the whole leaf. Why shouldn't you, who work hard to save every penny, follow their example? Cutting the core out of a head of iceberg lettuce can be wasteful also. An easy way to remove the core efficiently and without a knife is to take the head of lettuce in your hand, core side down, and to thump it really hard on a solid surface. The core can then be pried out easily with your fingers, minimizing waste.

Don't waste the peels. Peeling vegetables and fruits can cost you a lot of nutrients and money, as well as adding to your garbage. Unless you absolutely can't have peels in your recipe, try to save them by scrubbing the vegetables instead of peeling them. You may not want to use the peels in mashed potatoes, but French fries and potato wedges don't lose any appeal with their skins still on. Many excellent recipes for potato salad call for leaving on at least part of the peel. Consider the popularity of fast-food places that serve potato wedges, restaurants that serve baked potato skins, and commercial snacks that are made out of real potato skins. Does it make sense to pay restaurants and stores high prices for something you throw out?

Fruit peels go to waste, too. People pay premium prices for candied citrus peel used in fruitcakes and stollen at Christmastime, and for grated orange or lemon peel used in general baking. Orange and lemon peel can be used in potpourri, too. If you bake apple or pear pies, you probably use a paring knife to remove the peel. If you aren't an extremely proficient peeler, you probably remove a lot of the fruit underneath as well. Try using a vegetable peeler to remove the skin, a corer to remove the core, and the knife to cut up the apple. This method yields less waste.

Store food properly to extend its shelf life. If your area has pests that can get into things, you may want to keep items like flour, cornmeal, and sugar in the refrigerator or to invest in a good set of sealable containers to keep the pests out. Herbs and spices lose their flavor very quickly when stored near heat, and can be very expensive to replace. Take the time to learn—from a knowledgeable friend or from your reading—the best way to store different meats, breads, cereals, fruits and vegetables, and anything else you store, in order to maximize their efficient use and minimize their cost to you.

Store your food in reusable plastic containers or glass jars. Plastic wrap, plastic bags, and aluminum foil all cost money each time you use them. Reusable containers will keep food just as fresh and save you money in the long run. If you reuse glass jars, you're really getting your money's worth—not only from the product that came in the jar, but from the packaging as well. You are also being kinder to the environment because you are reducing the amount of garbage you generate.

Learn how to preserve food. Occasionally you can get a really special buy on fruits and vegetables you use a lot; it would be a shame if you had the money for this terrific buy but couldn't eat it before it spoiled. Canning, freezing, and drying are ways you can preserve food so you don't have to eat it all right away. Each method has its place, and each works better with certain types of foods. Home canning, for example, tends to work better with acidic foods like tomatoes, and you must learn the proper preparation procedures to avoid food poisoning. With some practice, and the right equipment, food preservation at home can save you hundreds of dollars each year. Store your canned or dried foods where they won't be exposed to sunlight, which can cause the taste and nutritional value of the food you worked so hard to preserve to deteriorate.

Cook your foods properly. Some people overcook their food, sacrificing all the good vitamins in the process; then they go out and spend more money on nutritional supplements. Baking or steaming your vegetables is better than boiling because many of the vitamins go down the drain with the boiling water. Baking and steaming also require less cooking oil than frying (or none at all), so you save money and add fewer calories and less fat.

Use the entire product. Quite often people will throw out a mayonnaise jar or catsup bottle because they think it's empty. In fact, there is usually enough of a product sticking to the sides to make another serving or two. Use a rubber spatula or bowl scraper to clean out wide-mouth jars. Turn narrow-mouth bottles upside down on a plate or in a bowl for about twenty minutes and let the contents trickle down (place them somewhere where they won't get tipped over easily). The contents can then be put into smaller, more accessible containers for future use.

Avoid wasting food at the dinner table. When you're serving a meal, give everyone, but especially kids, smaller initial servings. Sometimes large helpings overwhelm small children. They might have fun playing with their food and flinging it on the floor to signal when they're finished, but is that a smart use of your money? It would be cheaper to feed them only what they want and need, using the money you save for other, better utilized items. Older children and adults can always ask for or help themselves to additional servings.

After meals, clear off the table as soon as possible. Food left sitting on the table leads to nibbling and possible food spoilage, which of course can be costly.

Use less of ingredients like salt, sugar, and butter. These usually are not needed to the extent called for by recipes. The amount of salt, sugar, and fat we like in our foods is an acquired taste that can be altered with a little effort. In fact, most health-conscious people today are deliberately seeking to reduce their consumption of these items. People with high blood pressure should eat less salt, for example, and almost everyone would benefit from eating less saturated fat from butter or margarine. Sugar contributes to weight gain and tooth decay. Try a new recipe first as originally written, then gradually decrease the salt, sugar, and butter each time you make it. Just think, if you have four recipes that call for a cup of sugar, and you have only three cups, you can make them all if you can get by with three-fourths of a cup of sugar in each. Unsweetened drink mixes, for example, can be combined with two-thirds or three-fourths cup of sugar per envelope. You can accustom your family to the new taste by cutting down on the sugar gradually.

If you buy drink mixes with sugar in them, switch to the unsweetened ones; it's less expensive to add your own sugar.

Buy and use skim or powdered milk instead of whole or 2-percent milk. Unless you have someone in your household who needs to gain weight, or a small child who needs the fat content of the milk to feed his growing body, skim milk is a healthy alternative. Introduce the skim milk into your family's diet by mixing it with whole milk and gradually decreasing the amount of whole milk. Before you start mixing, though, begin storing your whole milk in a pitcher so the change will be less noticeable. One of our neighbors changed her family's milk without their knowledge. When her children came to our house, they refused to drink our skim milk. They didn't know that their mom had been serving skim milk to them for months!

Skim milk can also be used to extend other types of milk products, like buttermilk, chocolate milk, or eggnog. Experiment to find the best mixture for your taste. My husband and I have found that we can mix commercial eggnog and skim milk in equal proportions and still have a quality we like. Even if your family absolutely refuses to drink skim milk, you should buy powdered milk to use in recipes that do not call for whole milk. You can mix it as needed, and none of it goes to waste. Skim milk in powdered form needs no refrigeration and has a long shelf life if stored in a dry place.

Whenever possible, suggest a nice, cool glass of water instead of juice or a soft drink. Even if you buy bottled water, it is much less expensive than a soft drink or juice. Of course, milk and juices do have necessary vitamins, and you don't want to eliminate them from your balanced diet, but no one except the soft drink industry will be hurt if you can eliminate soft drinks from your menu. And think of how much money you can save!

If your family will drink juice but won't drink water, you can usually add more water to the frozen concentrate than the manufacturer prescribes. Instead of being juice, the beverage becomes a fruit drink or an ade. This method works best on single-fruit juices such as orange juice, grape juice, and lemonade. When you're dealing with mixed-fruit concentrates, it may be more difficult to add extra water without the resulting beverage tasting watered down. Again, experimentation is the best way to find out what works best for you and your family.

Stretch your spreadable foods. They will spread better and further at room temperature. Peanut butter is spreadable at its best at room temperature; it goes even further if it's creamy instead of chunky. At our house, we like those expensive cheese spreads. They often sell for about two dollars for eight ounces. We buy a package of cream cheese and mix it with the more expensive cheese for a milder flavor, and the combination goes twice as far for less money.

Purchase thin-sliced bread instead of regular slices. The thin-sliced loaf may offer only a few extra slices, but if you make a lot of sandwiches, as I do, it makes a difference.

Find ways to salvage foods that have changed texture but are still edible. Brown sugar, for example, tends to get rock hard, making it unusable. You can take care of this problem by sealing it in a plastic bag with a piece of bread. You will have a dry piece of bread after this process—but don't throw it away! Use it to make bread crumbs (see Creative Cooking, below). Similarly, you can revive soggy crackers and cereal; spread them out on a tray, and bake them in a toaster oven at the lowest setting for ten minutes or until they turn crisp again.

Creative Cooking

One reason a lot of food is wasted is because the food itself is boring. If you're throwing out food, you're watching your money go into the garbage. Avoid slipping into a culinary rut. Read cookbooks, trade recipes with friends, and—above all—use your own imagination to create exciting variations, either in the food itself, or in the atmosphere surrounding meals. For example, you could set aside one meal a week to clean out the refrigerator and let everyone choose which leftovers they want to eat. Since eating leftovers is not usually at the top of everyone's list of fun things to do, you might introduce a novel atmosphere centered around that meal: perhaps you could have an indoor "picnic" or eat by candlelight. Another possibility would be to encourage each member of the family to choose a leftover and see what scrumptious concoction he or she could come up with, with the winner being relieved of dishwashing chores that evening. Similarly, you might eat leftover steak or ham for breakfast, or you might pack leftovers in bag lunches and save the price of the meals that otherwise would be purchased from a canteen, snack bar, or restaurant.

A kitchen is like a chemistry lab. In both places, you have to measure and mix the right amounts of the proper ingredients to get the desired results. In the lab, an improper mixture may explode, while in a kitchen the worst thing that can happen is that you might produce an inedible dish. When I was growing up, my mother taught my siblings and me how to follow a recipe. My father taught us how to add different ingredients to make the original recipe more interesting. He also taught us the various properties of the ingredients so we would be able to substitute or make variations on our own. Of course, not all of our experimentation worked out perfectly, but we kept on trying.

Often it takes only small changes in your recipes to liven them up. These changes need not take a long time or cost a lot of money. With cookies, for instance, you can add chocolate chips, raisins, nuts, or extract—among other things—to change a basic recipe. These ingredients can be added individually or in any combination, resulting in a new type of cookie. Take a look at new products on the market and think about how you could make them at home. If you use a little imagination and common sense, you can use ordinary, inexpensive items to create novel food dishes that stimulate the appetite and prevent waste as well.

Another way to be creative and save money is to use up all the odds and ends in your cupboard when you cook. Most of us have boxes taking up space in our cupboards that have a few crackers, a little cereal, some instant potatoes, etc., in them that will soon become stale and eventually be thrown in the garbage. Many cookbooks have lists of suggested substitutes in case you don't have all the ingredients of a recipe on hand. Use these suggestions to help you determine how to make the best use of whatever odd ingredients you already have. The following are a number of suggested ways to put these odds and ends to use.

Use instant mashed potatoes instead of flour as a thickener for gravy or soup.

 If you have several varieties of leftover cereal, mix them together and serve them for breakfast or add them to a trail mix as an extender.

Employ unsweetened cereal, about-to-be-stale pota- to chips, or cracker crumbs as a coating mix for meat or as a substitute for bread in meat loaf.

Run leftover rolls, bread slices, or toast through the blender and turn them into bread crumbs, or toast them and cut them into cubes for croutons. Why throw the bread away and then pay for bread crumbs or croutons when you don't have to?

 Substitute orange juice for milk in waffles.

 Replace raisins with dried fruit.

 Use toasted oats in place of chopped nuts.

 Substitute yogurt or buttermilk for sour cream.

 Substitute one type of extract for another—use almond instead of vanilla, for instance.

 Switch to fruit baby food as a nutritious replacement for sugary ice cream toppings.

Use thinly sliced hot dogs in place of pepperoni on pizza.

 Combine meat drippings and a little cornstarch as a tasty alternative to commercial gravy.

Try serving waffles made from cake mix or ginger-bread for dessert. They are interesting, tasty, and quick to fix.

In some cases, you can use whole-grain or oatmeal flour in place of white flour. It may change the texture some, so substitute only up to one-third of the flour the recipe calls for.

Try mixing two cups of fruit juice, a prepared soft drink mix, or soda pop with a package of unflavored gelatin instead of making a three-ounce package of flavored commercial gelatin. (Don't substitute pineapple juice as the liquid, though, because the dessert might not congeal.)

Substitute cooked egg noodles spread on an un-greased pan for regular pizza crust dough.

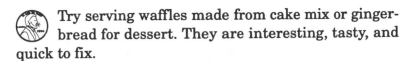 Replace ground beef with ground turkey in many dishes—like meat loaf, chili, and pasta sauces. Turkey costs less, is high in protein, and has less fat.

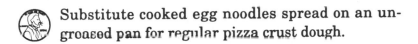 Try a different type of fowl in your poultry recipes. For instance, chicken can replace game hens, or turkey can be used in place of chicken.

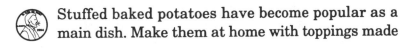 Stuffed baked potatoes have become popular as a main dish. Make them at home with toppings made

from leftover spaghetti sauce, gravy, vegetables, chili, ground beef, taco filling, etc. This way, leftovers that could have fed one person can feed three or four people.

Take advantage of the current popularity of salad bars. You can make a meal out of salad using some of the leftovers in your refrigerator, including leftover macaroni or potato salad, lettuce, scrambled eggs, vegetables, grated cheese, chopped lunch meat, and tuna. Taco salad makes use of leftover ground beef, cheese, and beans. A little salad dressing, oil and vinegar, or a yogurt dressing completes the salad.

When you don't have enough of any one ingredient, combine several to create an economical meal. If you have only one small can of chili and a lot of people to feed, cook macaroni and mix it with the chili. Top it with cheese. Cook a can of soup with enough rice to make it a rice dish instead of soup, or use noodles instead of rice. When you can't find enough of any one vegetable in your refrigerator to make a meal, stir-fry small portions of several vegetables and a small amount of meat to create a nutritious, delicious, and inexpensive meal. Mix gravy or soy sauce with the vegetables, and serve the mixture over noodles, rice, potatoes, or biscuits.

Explore creative options using cross-cultural cuisine. Use taco sauce and meat with lettuce and tomato on a hamburger bun. Blend sloppy joe fixings and taco shells with cheese and lettuce. Tortillas, French bread, pitas, or hamburger buns make good pizza crusts. If you slice hot dogs thinly and add them to macaroni, you have a meat dish for several people.

Since the most expensive part of any dinner is the meat, chicken, or seafood in the main course, create dishes that use meat, chicken, or seafood as *part* of the main dish, with pasta, bread crumbs, potatoes, rice, and other foods as the larger ingredient. Since you will need less of the more expensive items, you will save money and feed more people. When you cut meat or other expensive ingredients into smaller pieces, it looks as if there is more of that ingredient in your dish. With casseroles, the only limit to the exciting dishes you can create is your willingness to experiment. You should also explore using vegetable- and grain-based main dishes. And don't forget the versatility of sandwiches, muffins, and omelettes as inexpensive meal alternatives.

A majority of Americans consider our nation's economy, and especially their family's or individual financial well-being, the number one issue confronting us today. Yet many people do not have the resolve, or will not take the time, to manage their spending. This lack of discipline is nowhere more apparent than in the way most of us shop for groceries: haphazardly, as if our expenditures for groceries were insignificant.

Relatively few people are concerned enough about what they spend on groceries to be willing to dedicate time and energy to managing their food purchases, food storage, and food preparation. The suggestions I have made are in no way intended to restrict your own initiative; there are a virtually unlimited number of ways to spend less, waste less, and enjoy more. Once you have applied your imagination to the guidelines above, perhaps you will discover more wonderful ways to pinch your grocery pennies.

4

Looking Good for Less

Food, clothing, and shelter are the three basic necessities of life, and certainly most of your income will be allocated to these essentials. Yet even within these three top-priority categories of your budget, there can be significant personal leeway in deciding how your money will be spent. You might consider food most important, for example, and focus on buying the most nutritious and appetizing food you can afford; or you might choose to sacrifice some quality or variety in food in order to possess a fine home. On the other hand, perhaps you feel that food and shelter aren't nearly as important as your personal appearance.

Although clothes are a basic necessity for warmth and for protection from the elements, to many people they represent much more. Because most people want to look their best, catering to the population's sense of fashion and personal appearance has become a multibillion-dollar business. In fact, the implication all around us—in advertising, the entertainment industry, even the business world—is that success in romance, in our jobs, and in life itself depends to a great extent on how we look. As a result, many consumers spend a great deal of time, energy, and money on clothing and on their personal appearance. It is possible, however, to look your best without spending a fortune on clothing and beauty products. Sometimes stretching your clothing dollar may mean altering your expectations and using your ingenuity, but you *can* look attractive and spend less.

YOUR WARDROBE

The key to making the most of your clothing dollars—as with all other aspects of managing your money—is taking stock of your resources and planning ahead. Never buy clothes on impulse; instead, always check what you already have in your closet and dresser and figure out what you absolutely need to give your current wardrobe a little more life. Then, using your budget as a guide, determine how much of your income you can allocate for clothing. Make a list of the items you want and put them in priority order. For example, if little Jimmy simply *must* have new shoes to go to school, and you only have twenty-five dollars to spend on clothes this month, then obviously his shoes take priority over that fancy dress you had your heart set on. Also, be sure to explore alternatives to purchasing new clothing that might stretch your dollars. Keep in mind the following.

Investigate alternatives to buying new clothes. Children's clothing, for example, can be very expensive, especially if you give in to their desire for designer labels. Children outgrow their clothes or wear them out in no time, so buying expensive outfits for them isn't worth the money. Instead, look for sales on clothes that you know are durable. There are also many alternative sources for children's clothing, like Goodwill or Salvation Army stores. Garage sales often have barely worn clothing on sale for great prices.

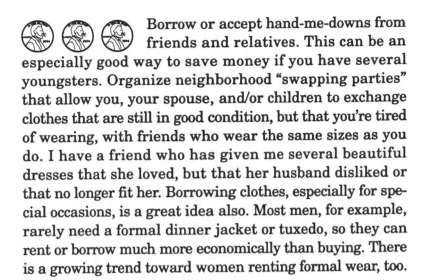 Borrow or accept hand-me-downs from friends and relatives. This can be an especially good way to save money if you have several youngsters. Organize neighborhood "swapping parties" that allow you, your spouse, and/or children to exchange clothes that are still in good condition, but that you're tired of wearing, with friends who wear the same sizes as you do. I have a friend who has given me several beautiful dresses that she loved, but that her husband disliked or that no longer fit her. Borrowing clothes, especially for special occasions, is a great idea also. Most men, for example, rarely need a formal dinner jacket or tuxedo, so they can rent or borrow much more economically than buying. There is a growing trend toward women renting formal wear, too.

Learn to make your own clothing or find a family member or close friend who sews. Clothes purchased from stores cost more than it would cost you to make clothes of similar quality at home. Another advantage to sewing is that you aren't limited to the selections on the store rack; you can choose the material and style that suits your tastes. If you're not experienced, you can find simple patterns especially designed for the beginner. When you become more experienced, you can modify patterns for your individual style. Look for patterns that you'll use more than once. If you can buy a $3.50 pattern and use it for two garments, the cost of the pattern per use is cut in half. To make your patterns last through several uses, don't use a tracing wheel with teeth on it to mark your fabric, and transfer patterns as soon as possible onto more durable paper, such as butcher paper. Shop carefully, and you may be able to find great bargains on remnant tables in fabric stores (but always measure

remnants to make sure they are big enough for your needs).
If a relative or friend will be doing the sewing, you can buy
the pattern and enough material for comparable clothing
for him or her in return for the labor.

In addition to finding alternative sources of
clothing, recycle the clothes you already own.
If your kids have shirts with absolutely no elbows or pants
with no knees, cut off and hem the garments slightly above
the damaged area and turn them into short-sleeved shirts
or shorts. If you have a run in one leg of your pantyhose,
don't immediately throw them away. Cut off the damaged
leg and wear the pantyhose with another pair that has the
opposite leg removed. You get a little extra tummy support, and your pantyhose get a longer life. Most men can
benefit from buying white athletic socks and just a few
basic colors—black, brown, and dark blue—of the same
style of dress sock; that way, when a sock wears thin or
develops a hole, the remaining spare can be easily matched
up as an extra.

Men, if you wear a necktie and inevitably end up
using it as a napkin or bib, purchase and use a can
of tie spray. Silk ties especially are almost impossible to
clean without wrinkling, but once sprayed with food and
drink repellent, a tie will wipe clean, eliminating the need
to dry clean or replace it (unless you have a major cata-
strophe, of course).

If you determine that you really have no option
but to purchase new clothes, shop around for
bargains. This means that you must know the regular
retail prices of different items. Many consumers buy clothes

only at discount stores or on sale at department stores. Some major stores have clearance centers or bargain basements that sell seconds, discontinued items, or things that are out of season. Also quite popular in many regions of the country are manufacturers' outlet stores. However, don't assume that you are finding the best deal just because you shop in an outlet or other discount store. The merchandise may be damaged beyond what is practical, it may be mistagged for size and quality, or it may actually cost more than in a regular retail store. If a garment is labelled as "irregular" or "second," check it over thoroughly to see if you can spot the flaw and if it is likely to affect the fit or wear of the garment. Try it on, check the seams, and look at the fasteners. Often the flaw is so small or so nearly invisible that you can't find it, in which case—if the price is right—the item might be an excellent bargain. Also, check on return policies, because sometimes bargain clothes can't be returned. As with all other smart shopping, there is no substitute for educating yourself through experience and by networking with other shoppers.

Purchase new clothes only at the end of the current season. In most cases, the season ends sooner in the store than it does for the consumer, anyway. Swimsuits, for example, usually go on sale after the Fourth of July. Stores want to clear their shelves to prepare for the next season. It's to their advantage to sell the merchandise for less now rather than to have to inventory it and store it until next year. Plan ahead for what you'll need. If you'll need a new winter coat, save some money by buying it when it's on sale. Buying for the next year is especially good if you have children; you can buy winter gear a size or two larger for the next year and put it away until the kids grow into it.

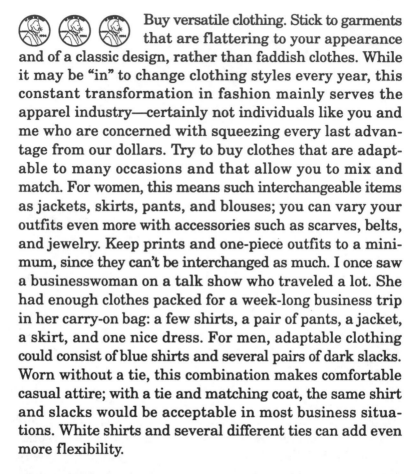 Buy versatile clothing. Stick to garments that are flattering to your appearance and of a classic design, rather than faddish clothes. While it may be "in" to change clothing styles every year, this constant transformation in fashion mainly serves the apparel industry—certainly not individuals like you and me who are concerned with squeezing every last advantage from our dollars. Try to buy clothes that are adaptable to many occasions and that allow you to mix and match. For women, this means such interchangeable items as jackets, skirts, pants, and blouses; you can vary your outfits even more with accessories such as scarves, belts, and jewelry. Keep prints and one-piece outfits to a minimum, since they can't be interchanged as much. I once saw a businesswoman on a talk show who traveled a lot. She had enough clothes packed for a week-long business trip in her carry-on bag: a few shirts, a pair of pants, a jacket, a skirt, and one nice dress. For men, adaptable clothing could consist of blue shirts and several pairs of dark slacks. Worn without a tie, this combination makes comfortable casual attire; with a tie and matching coat, the same shirt and slacks would be acceptable in most business situations. White shirts and several different ties can add even more flexibility.

When you are planning your budget for clothes, be realistic in judging your size and tendency to gain or lose weight. A wardrobe of classic clothing will only be useful if it fits you. Changing sizes, whether you're gaining or losing weight, means buying new clothes. While you might have the best intentions in the world, don't purchase all those two-sizes-smaller clothes until *after* you have maintained your own smaller size for at least six months.

Use the appropriate cleaning methods. Once you have purchased your clothes, you want to make them last as long as possible, which means keeping them clean and in good repair. *Before* you buy, examine labels and consider how each item of clothing needs to be cleaned. Dry cleaning can become very expensive. Garments with fur or leather on them are very expensive to clean, too. One-hundred-percent cotton items, while extremely comfortable, tend to shrink when washed, so if you can predict frequent washings, you might consider buying clothes made of wash-and-wear polyester/cotton blends for most of your wardrobe.

To avoid wearing holes in the knees of pants, put patches on the inside of new pants where they would normally wear out. Children's clothing can have colorful patches put on the outside as well. When I was little, my mother had to mend my favorite sweatshirt, which had a hole in it. It required a patch, but the patch would have been obvious, so she took out some of her small cookie cutters and made a few animal-shaped patches and scattered them around on the front of my sweatshirt. With the patches, my sweatshirt became a fashion statement.

If you buy heavy coats with buttons that will be under a lot of stress, reinforce the sewing with coat thread or dental floss. Both are heavier and more durable than regular sewing thread.

Don't overdry your clothes. Remember, all that lint in your lint filter is coming from your clothes, making the material thinner. Overdrying also causes your clothes to shrink more and elastic to deteriorate faster, as well as using energy needlessly.

Select shoes that are comfortable, durable, and functional rather than fashionable. Most of us have one pair of shoes that we almost live in, while the rest just sit in the closet and collect dust. Perhaps more than any other item of clothing, shoes serve a practical purpose in addition to covering up part of our body: They should fit the feet and provide support for the sometimes difficult task of holding us upright. Women in particular tend to be masochists when it comes to footwear. We'll put up with a lot of pain and strain to wear pretty shoes that are expensive and not particularly functional. Before buying those pretty shoes, ask yourself how they will feel on your feet after you've been standing for ten hours or walking a few blocks. You may decide you don't really need them after all.

Buy shoes in the middle of the day. Your feet swell a little by midday, and you don't want to end up with shoes that are too tight. Make sure you try on the shoes with the type of stockings or socks you intend to wear with them.

When buying shoes, try both shoes on and walk around to see if they're comfortable. Shoe sizes vary among manufacturers, and since most people try on the right shoe, it can be stretched and not as tight as the left. Another reason to try on both shoes is that both of your feet aren't exactly the same size. A shoe may feel fine on one foot while its mate pinches the other foot.

To make your new shoes last longer, look at the shoes you're replacing and see where they're worn. You may be able to prevent excessive wear by buying things like heel protectors for the new shoes.

Resist the temptation to buy children fancy shoes at fancy prices. Children don't always need the most expensive shoes around. Unless your child has especially wide feet or an orthopedic problem, a well-made pair of sneakers will usually be fine for everyday wear. And don't let your children make you feel guilty because you won't buy them the $200 shoes that supposedly will make them fly or dance (or whatever) like that sports or television star in the advertisements. Remember, it's the advertiser's job to sell you a product; it's your task to resist unless the product turns out to be worth the hype. With children's shoes—since children can easily outgrow a pair in two or three months—it's especially important that you be cautious. If you don't allow for extra space, you'll end up spending excessive time and money in the shoe store.

Mix accessories to vary your wardrobe. Jewelry, scarves, ties, suspenders, belts, hats, and vests can really add mileage to your wardrobe. If your budget allows, use accessories to match your mood and enhance your appearance. For the most part, expensive accessories—like jewelry—should not take up very much of your budget until you reach a time when your income is more than adequate. If you do look at jewelry, though, make sure you understand exactly what's being offered. The purity of gold, for instance, is measured in karats. Only 24-karat gold is pure gold; any lesser number means that the gold has been mixed with a less expensive metal (the lower the number, the less gold it contains). And did you know that "faux" is really just the French word for "fake?"

Everyone is familiar with the old saw, "The clothes make the man," but I prefer to turn this cliche around. To me, the individual underneath is vastly more important than the clothes he or she wears. Try to cultivate an affirmative attitude about yourself, and the world around you, and you will to a great extent determine the way everyone else perceives you. The most expensive clothing from posh shops on several continents will not make a dour, offensive person attractive; on the other hand, we all know humble souls who could wear jeans and tattered shirts almost anywhere and fit right in because of their positive attitude.

YOUR APPEARANCE

Perhaps nowhere else in the world are people as obsessed with their personal appearance and hygiene as in the United States of America. Part of this concern is quite beneficial in that it leads individuals to protect their health by eating properly, exercising, and maintaining sanitary living conditions. Another part of this concern is excessive, however, and breeds guilt, shame, and feelings of inadequacy in those who feel that they can't measure up to society's standards of personal beauty, however unrealistic and even false they may be.

If you are tempted to spend a lot of money you can't afford on your personal appearance, examine your self-image. My advice to you is, "You appear as you are." First, follow the advice of Socrates to examine and "know thyself." Second, learn to like yourself. If there are parts of your appearance you can easily change, and if it's important to you, by all means change them. But if the parts you don't like are things that you can't change, focus on learning to like yourself the way you are. Once you do, other people will like you better, too. And unlike fancy clothes and beauty aids, neither of these efforts will cost you the first penny! Once you have learned to accept yourself, the following suggestions will make sense.

If you spend a lot of money keeping your hair looking good, consider learning how to cut your own hair. Better still, get together with a friend or relative and *both* learn to cut hair. Then you can take turns doing each other's hair. Before you know it, in addition to getting free haircuts, you might be making money trimming the neighbors' hair, too.

If learning to cut hair isn't feasible, try visiting a cosmetology or barber school to have students cut your hair. Students, supervised by their instructors, will often give you a good haircut for a reasonable price. Some haircutting chains offer free haircuts at certain times of the year, if they run schools. Ask around.

Be wary of exaggerated promises made by the makers of cosmetics, shampoos, and other beauty aids. Many advertisements imply that products will dramatically improve your appearance, make you look younger, and so on. Many of these items claim to contain special ingredients and secret formulas, for which you pay exorbitant amounts of money. In fact, you'll find the same key ingredients in most product families. If you look at the labels of moisturizing creams, for example, you'll find that the largest component of most of them is petrolatum (petroleum jelly). Other ingredients are added mainly to give each brand a different texture or scent. If you use an expensive moisturizing cream, chances are you can find one with essentially the same ingredients that costs much less. Similarly, astringents or "toners" are all basically mixtures of alcohol and water, with scent added. You can get the same effect far more economically by using witch hazel (aqua hamamelis) or, if your skin is very dry, mixing equal amounts of witch hazel and distilled water to make a soothing, nondrying toning lotion.

Many shampoos come with directions to lather your hair twice. In fact, the second soaping only uses more shampoo and a few extra minutes of your time. You can cut your shampoo use in half, and still have clean hair, by lathering well once instead of twice.

In general, use as few cosmetic "helpers" as possible. Because of all the advertising and packaging involved in cosmetics, you always end up paying for the image, not the product. Remember, the more you smile, the fewer cosmetics you'll need. Not only will you look better when you're smiling, but you're using only one-fifth as many muscles as it takes to frown, and if you smile a lot your face will still look happy when it's in repose. This can save many firming-cream sales in the future.

Use natural alternatives to manufactured products. Lemon juice and buttermilk are natural banishing agents and can eliminate unwanted freckles. Cucumber slices or tea bags can be great for puffy eyes. Beer or eggs can be good for your hair. A sage tea rinse will make your hair darker; lemon juice will make it lighter. Many salad ingredients can work as facial treatments. (The only problem is that most of these items are perishable once prepared, so you can't mix up large quantities.)

When shopping for cosmetics, look for companies that provide samples or will give a refund or exchange if you're not satisfied. Two such companies are Avon and Jafra. If you try a demonstrator on in a department store, don't use it on your face. Try it on your hand or arm to see if it will change color when it comes in contact with your skin.

Keep lipsticks and blush sticks in the refrigerator to help them last longer. If your lipstick is warm, a lot more comes off on your lips. A cooler tube allows you to use only as much as you want so it will go further. You can also use lipstick to double as a blush. This way, you get a perfect match without having to spend extra money for blush to match each lipstick. A friend of mine has gotten a number of compliments by using this technique.

When nail polish becomes a little thick, add a drop or two of polish remover to the bottle, and you can continue using the polish.

Don't store cosmetics in the bathroom. The warm, damp climate of the bathroom allows bacteria to grow faster, thus shortening the effective life span of the cosmetics. In any case, discard eye makeup after three or four months. Bacteria builds up, and you could get a serious eye infection.

Store perfume or cologne in a cool, dark place for longer life. Heat and sunlight can change the fragrance very quickly.

Use perfumes and colognes sparingly, and buy cologne instead of perfume. Cologne has an alcohol content of about 22 percent, while perfume has a 15- to 18-percent alcohol content. The next time you shop, notice the price difference for that 4- to 7-percent difference. For men, cologne is usually more expensive (but less necessary) than after-shave. Plain rubbing alcohol or witch hazel, which are inexpensive, make excellent after-shave. With just a drop of added cologne, alcohol can replace both after-shave and the expensive fragrance.

Since both are less expensive than cologne or perfume, let talc or soap serve as your fragrance. Soap can be put in your drawer as a sachet as well as being used in your bath.

Since most cosmetics will last two years if they're not opened, buy only what you can realistically use within the next two years.

Remember, with all cosmetics, a little goes a long way. One matchmaking expert said recently that men aren't attracted to women who wear excessive jewelry, makeup, or fragrance. I know many women who would rather avoid men who overdo their fragrance also. Most often we can save money on cosmetics by just using less.

To stay in shape, instead of paying large sums of money to join a spa or fitness center, exercise at home. Forget about the tummy slimmers, the expensive rowing machines, and most of the other pieces of apparatus that are supposed to make you sexy and romantic. A good pair of walking shoes is all the equipment you need, and it is well worth the cost. It costs you nothing (except a few calories, which is the whole point) to walk around the block. Walking up stairs is one of the best aerobic exercises you can perform.

Caution: Before starting any exercise program for the first time, depending on your age and the general state of your health, it may be wise to consult a doctor. Always begin with a moderate pace and amount of exercise; then gradually increase your performance as your body becomes accustomed to a routine.

While it is certainly true that your appearance, including the clothes you wear, plays a role in determining how other people perceive you—and how you perceive yourself—its importance is vastly overrated by our Madison Avenue-dominated society. Don't allow the advertising media to sell you on the mistaken notion that you can't be happy—or successful—without spending hundreds or thousands of dollars on your appearance. You can look great for a lot less than that. And the real you—the you that is resolved to get ahead in this world—realizes that it's your inner spirit that really counts. So keep pinching those pennies, and count the dollars and the days until you can have everything that you ever wanted.

5
Home Economics: Saving Money on Housing and Household Management

You now know ways to pinch pennies on your food and clothing expenses. The third basic necessity of life is shelter, and the expenses involved in providing shelter are a substantial part of any personal budget. Although the amount may vary significantly, depending on individual needs, 25 percent or more of a family's income will be spent on housing; therefore, saving money on housing can have a major impact on your budget. If you are like most people, you will start out renting an apartment or small house. Sooner or later, usually after you have developed stable employment and income, you will be confronted with the decision of whether you want to continue renting or to try to buy your own home. Of course, each alternative has advantages and disadvantages.

RENTAL HOUSING

Rental housing is usually accessible and convenient; you don't have to worry about repairs, and if you decide to move, you don't have to worry about selling a house or an apartment. If you rent, you don't have to worry about property taxes or mortgage payments, and your monthly rental may be less than house payments would be. On the other hand, you have to be careful with the landlord's property, and you need to ask permission to make any alterations or improvements. There may be restrictions on the number of children you can have living with you, and pets may be disallowed entirely.

If you rent, one of the smartest things you can do is to become aware of your rights as a tenant. This can help you avoid costly arguments with the landlord. Here are some things you can do before you move in that will help prevent problems later.

Check to see what your rights are as a renter before you begin looking for rental housing. The Fair Housing Office should be able to give you the information you need. Look in the government pages in your phone book.

When you look at an apartment or house, take note of every nick, dent, and scratch. Make sure EVERYTHING works properly. If you're really interested in renting, bring a friend as a witness or take pictures (with the landlord in them if possible). If you don't document every flaw, you may end up losing some or all of your security deposit to repair damage that existed before you moved in.

Remember, you must have the landlord's permission to make any alterations. If you just go ahead and do them yourself, or if you don't receive permission, you're leaving yourself open to possible legal action. If any repairs or alterations need to be done on the property, make sure you notify your landlord in writing and keep a copy of your letter. You must also keep any correspondence you receive from your landlord. The correspondence is proof of any agreements. Phone calls are not good enough, since the landlord can always say later that he didn't agree. Always reinforce phone calls and other oral agreements *in writing*.

   If you decide to rent a property, make sure you know exactly what's contained in the rental agreement. Courts generally will enforce any lease agreement that you enter into voluntarily—even if you discover later that you are being taken advantage of— and many leases require you to pay any legal fees involved in disputes between you and the landlord. If you object to part of an agreement's wording, state your complaints *before* you sign, not afterward. We realized one month before we had our second child that the lease we had signed specified residency by two adults and one child. The management had changed since we signed the lease, and the new manager was unaware of my condition. We checked with him to see if we would have to move or if the rent would be raised when the new baby came. The answer surprised us. First, the owner said he didn't want four people living in a two-bedroom apartment. When we pointed out that six people were living in the apartment across from us, the landlord said that we would be still evicted if the new baby was a girl because, according to rules stated in the lease, unmarried males and females were not permitted to share a bedroom. This meant that if we had a little girl, she would have to have a separate bedroom from her brother. We had to move in a hurry, and the day after we moved, our daughter made her debut.

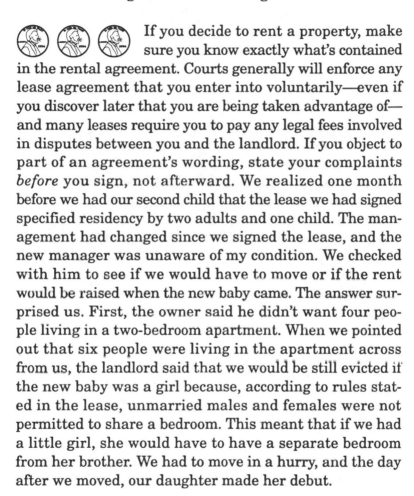 Ask questions and seek legal advice if you feel it is necessary. Many attorneys

are willing to grant a free or inexpensive initial consultation. You might be much better off to spend a few dollars before you sign a lease than to get trapped in a no-win situation. For example, many times a lease may bind you to making rental payments even if you are forced to move out before the lease expires.

Find out if your landlord can sell the property during the period of the lease. If the landlord decides to sell, and you're still living in the property, conditions can become intolerable quickly. For example, some landlords will leave a key with a realtor or attach a lock box to the house so that real estate agents can show the property to prospective buyers—without your permission or prior knowledge. You might be embarrassed by someone walking into your living quarters while you're sleeping or taking a shower. You should also find out how much time you will be allowed to move if the property is sold. Moving is traumatic and expensive enough without the additional aggravation of finding another place on short notice.

Don't sign *any* agreement with empty spaces or a signature line that isn't right under the last line of the contract. Information can be filled in later by an unscrupulous landlord, so it's best to eliminate that possibility.

Be prepared to put down a security and cleaning deposit equal to a month's rent; you may also have to pay at least one month's rent in advance. Before putting down a deposit, however, make sure you determine whether it is returnable, and what conditions you must meet to have it returned.

Make sure you get a copy of any settlement statement, and that the terms are acceptable. When you move out, the landlord will inspect the property, and both you and the landlord should sign a statement as to whether or not the condition of the property was acceptable to the landlord. Fourteen days later, you should receive either a refund of your deposit or an itemized list of how it was spent to repair damage to the property. My husband and I once lost a damage deposit and had to fight for almost two months to get an itemized statement of the expenses. We had signed a paper stating the house was in acceptable condition when we left, but our carbon copy was unreadable, and we weren't able to get a good copy. As a result, we ended up paying for cleaning a house that was already clean and for repairing appliances that we never used. I later checked with the new tenants and found out that none of these things had been done. Unfortunately, it would have cost more to take the landlord to court than our deposit was worth.

HOME OWNERSHIP

Once you have decided to live in a particular area and have settled into a job, you should begin to check out the advantages of home ownership. For most people, one of the most wonderful feelings in the world is the pride in having that special place to call your own—a home you can fix up any way you please so that it expresses your unique personality. The traditional American Dream centers around owning a home. It doesn't have to be big, or fancy, or expensive, just so long as it's yours.

But there is more to home ownership than personal satisfaction; there are some real economic benefits also. When you pay monthly rent, the entire amount is gone forever;

you don't have anything to show for your money except the privilege of staying on—if the landlord agrees. For about the same monthly payment as your rent, sometimes even less, you might be able to live in your own home!

The United States government subsidizes, or helps, you in buying a home, by means of tax breaks. For example, all the money you pay for local property taxes is deductible when you compute your federal income taxes, and in most states it is deductible from state taxes as well. In addition, you can deduct all of the interest you pay on your home mortgage. Since almost all of your payments will go for interest for at least half of the duration of your mortgage, you will have a substantial tax deduction for many years, which can be viewed as extra income. For example, let's say you and your spouse make $35,000 per year and pay $500 a month rent. You manage to come up with a down payment on a house and qualify for a mortgage of $84,000, with a monthly payment of $713. At first glance, your mortgage payment would seem to be $213 more per month than your rent was. However, the entire $713 you pay each month goes for interest on the loan and is tax-deductible, as is the $1,000 you pay for property tax. If you are in a 25-percent tax bracket, these deductions will save you $2,389 per year, or $199 per month, in income taxes. So for just $14 per month more than you were paying in rent ($213 more in the monthly payment less the $199 reduction in taxes) you (and the bank) now own your own home! These figures will vary, depending on your interest rate, the terms of your mortgage, and your tax bracket, but the point is valid regardless: In most instances, there are valid economic reasons why you should consider purchasing rather than renting your home.

Perhaps an even greater financial advantage of home

ownership is that houses, unlike cars and clothes and furniture, tend to appreciate in value. During times of high inflation this appreciation can be considerable; thus, the house you purchase today for $60,000—with normal upkeep and care—may be worth over $70,000 in four or five years. Of course, there are no guarantees that the value of your house will increase, and you need to learn everything you can about your local real estate market before you purchase property, but for the most part buying your own home can be financially rewarding. Meanwhile, you will enjoy the benefits of living in your own place with your own style.

Making the Decision

If you are interested in buying your own home, your first step should be to talk with some of your friends or relatives who own or are buying homes. Find out what kinds of problems they have encountered, and ask if they recommend taking the action. Then—*before* you begin looking around to find that dream home—analyze your finances to determine what you can afford, and how much you need to save to raise a down payment. Don't let your bank tell you that you can't prequalify for a loan. We tried numerous banks and were told we had to pick out a house first and then find out if we would be accepted for a mortgage. So we went out three times and found nice houses, each priced lower than the last, but each time we were told we didn't qualify for the loan. Finally, we found one we could afford. It would have been much easier if the bank had just let us know how much we could afford before we started looking.

If you cannot convince a bank to prequalify you, use the rule of thumb that you can expect to spend, in addition to a down payment (usually 10 to 20 percent of the total price) 30 percent of your gross income to pay for a home (see Table 5.1).

Keep in mind that buying a home must fit into your overall financial plan. Once you have a rough idea of what you can afford to pay in mortgage payments, insurance, and property taxes, you can then plug these figures into your budget and see how they work. If you discover, for example, that after the mortgage payment there would be no money remaining for food or clothes, then your decision is fairly obvious. In most cases, however, you will find that replacing the rent payment with a mortgage payment will require only a few dollars more per month. Then your decision becomes more difficult: You must decide where you can find the extra money, which usually means deciding what you can sacrifice. Are you willing to give up eating meals out? Are you willing to drive that old clunker for two more years? What about buying fewer clothes and toys for your kids so that they can live in a home of their own? These are tough decisions that you and all the members of your family should discuss together. The information in Table 5.1 should be helpful to you in making your decision, but remember that each situation is unique, and there is no substitute for going out and learning on your own.

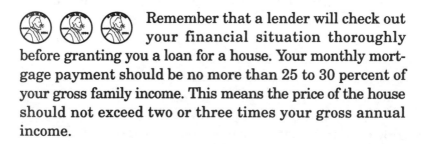 Remember that a lender will check out your financial situation thoroughly before granting you a loan for a house. Your monthly mortgage payment should be no more than 25 to 30 percent of your gross family income. This means the price of the house should not exceed two or three times your gross annual income.

Table 5.1 Amount Available for Monthly Mortgage Payment at 30 Percent of Gross Income

Annual Gross Income	Monthly Gross Income	Available for Payment
$15,000	$1,250	$ 375
$20,000	$1,667	$ 500
$25,000	$2,083	$ 625
$30,000	$2,500	$ 750
$35,000	$2,917	$ 875
$40,000	$3,333	$1,000
$45,000	$3,750	$1,125
$50,000	$4,167	$1,250

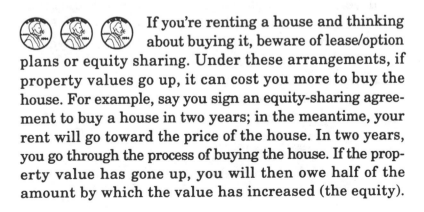 When you're calculating the cost of buying a home, also consider closing costs, which—along with the down payment—must be paid at the time of closing. Closing costs can include homeowner's insurance, mortgage insurance, prepayments for property taxes, and other fees; typically these costs average 3 to 4 percent of the loan amount.

If you're renting a house and thinking about buying it, beware of lease/option plans or equity sharing. Under these arrangements, if property values go up, it can cost you more to buy the house. For example, say you sign an equity-sharing agreement to buy a house in two years; in the meantime, your rent will go toward the price of the house. In two years, you go through the process of buying the house. If the property value has gone up, you will then owe half of the amount by which the value has increased (the equity).

Thus, if the house was worth $50,000 two years ago and is now worth $60,000, you will now have to pay $55,000 to buy the house. Worse, you may not be able to qualify for the loan for the new price.

If you're seriously looking for a house, take a businesslike attitude. Examine houses carefully and know what you're looking at. You can check for simple things like obvious water leaks, cracked paint, or broken fixtures. You may want an engineer to look for more serious structural problems. Pay special attention to signs of cracking foundations, termite damage, poor water pressure (which may be a sign that the pipes are corroded), dimming lights (which may indicate that the electrical system is overloaded and needs to be rewired), and inefficient or poorly working heating or cooling systems. If major repairs are called for, take them into consideration before you make an offer. Remember, the homeowners will be anxious to sell, so don't expect them to voluntarily tell you everything that is wrong.

By all means work through a realtor, especially if you have never bought a home before. Although real estate agents or brokers are expensive, in most cases their commission (usually 6 percent or more) is paid by the seller, not by the buyer. Of course, you may wind up paying a higher price for the house because of the commission, but this is often negotiable, and in any case the broker's experience can sometimes save you from even more costly errors. In the long run, a good broker will save you time and money. He or she will know about the quality of the neighborhood, the proximity of schools and shopping areas, zoning restrictions, and many other things that are crucial to your choice of a home. In addition, the broker will work with you and the seller to facilitate the purchasing process, and will normally set up the closing with you and your lending institution. Ask around and find out which agents are recommended as the most knowledgeable and trustworthy.

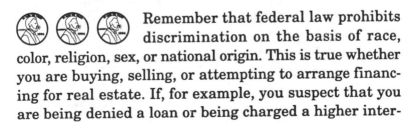 Even with the services of a broker, however, you must take the final responsibility for the purchase. Learn as much as you can about the value of homes in your area, and discuss with your family the most important qualities you are looking for in a home. Will you be living in this house for many years, or do you plan to move in a year or so? Do you want to be within walking distance of the nearest schools? What is the neighborhood like? Perhaps you would prefer to buy a small condominium, with less maintenance to worry about and access to a swimming pool or tennis courts. Are you willing and able to trade a lot of your time and energy fixing up an older house, or one in need of serious repairs? If so, you might save money and turn your "sweat equity" into dollars that could be used for other purchases. Make a list of your priorities and write down an appraisal of each house you visit; that way, you won't forget as easily which houses made the best impression (see A House-Hunting Checklist, page 104).

Remember that federal law prohibits discrimination on the basis of race, color, religion, sex, or national origin. This is true whether you are buying, selling, or attempting to arrange financing for real estate. If, for example, you suspect that you are being denied a loan or being charged a higher inter-

A House-Hunting Checklist

Copy this checklist to use as a guide when you visit houses. If there are other considerations that you feel are important, add them in the space provided.

House	Superior	Average	Poor
Size (square feet)			
Number of bedrooms			
Baths			
Closets/storage			
Kitchen			
Basement/garage			
Plumbing/heating			
Roof			
Interior condition			
Exterior condition			
Lawn/size of lot			
Neighborhood			
Condition of nearby homes			
Traffic/noise			
Security/safety			
Zoning			
Convenience			
Work			
Schools/child care			
Shopping/grocery stores			
Parks and recreation			
Hospitals/health care			
Transportation/airport			
Fire/police protection			
Other			

est rate because of your race or sex, you can make a formal complaint to the office of Housing and Urban Development in Washington, D.C.

Buying Your Home

When buying a home, you should shop for a home mortgage just as you would shop for any other major purchase: Learn as much as you can about your options, take your time, keep an open mind, and be flexible. There are many factors to consider, including the interest rate, the length of the mortgage, and the amount of the down payment; each of these will have an effect on the size of your monthly payment. For each 1-percent increase in the interest rate, for example, the annual income required to manage the repayment schedule rises by about $2,500. Similarly, the number of years you borrow the money significantly affects the interest costs you must repay. And interest rates vary from bank to bank, so shop around.

There are three basic types of mortgages. A *conventional mortgage* is one given on a home for a long period of time, usually twenty-five or thirty years, and for a fixed interest rate (that is, the interest rate remains the same for the life of the loan). You must make a substantial down payment, usually 20 percent of the price of the home. Since your monthly payment stays the same over the life of the loan, assuming your income increases over the years, the payment will take up a decreasing percentage of your budget over time.

A *variable-rate mortgage*, or *adjustable-rate mortgage* (ARM), allows the lender to raise or lower interest rates based on a certain predefined index (like the United States Treasury Securities Index) that fluctuates according to the general state of the nation's economy. Usually there is a "cap," or maximum amount the rate can be increased, regardless of the economy, and the rate does decrease when interest rates decline. An ARM is usually easier to obtain and has a lower initial rate than other conventional mortgages, but since the rate can increase, many people prefer the predictability of a fixed-rate mortgage.

Government-guaranteed loans include those backed by the Federal Housing Administration (FHA) and by the Department of Veterans' Affairs (VA). In general, FHA and VA loans, since they are guaranteed by the United States government, require lower down payments than conventional mortgages or ARMs. (Typically an FHA loan requires only a 5-percent down payment, or even 3 percent, instead of the 20 percent for a conventional mortgage.) However, there are additional, rather strict, regulations that the borrower must follow. For example, if you're buying through a VA or FHA loan, the house itself has to qualify for the loan. If it needs repairs, it may be rejected. You should insist on the repairs, however, if you really want the house. Repairs that are pointed out by VA or FHA representatives aren't frivolous. You can have a contract written up saying you will buy the house only if all required repairs are done. Make sure each specific repair is listed before you sign.

When a mortgage lender forecloses on a loan insured by the FHA, the United States Department of Housing and Urban Development (HUD) pays off the loan and acquires possession of the property. HUD then offers the house for sale to the general public at fair market value. Ask your realtor about HUD houses in your area, because there are many advantages to buying from HUD. Many HUD homes require only a 3-percent down payment, and HUD may pay closing costs (which average 3 to 4 percent of the price of your home) and the realtor's commission.

After you have carefully selected your home and your lender, you are ready to make an offer. When your offer is accepted, you are ready for the closing—in which you, your realtor, the lender, and your attorney sit down to sign the important papers. Here are a few tips to keep in mind.

Try not to be nervous. If you have examined your options and worked closely with a trustworthy realtor, you're making the right decision. Your realtor should warn you about what important papers to bring to the closing.

Close on the house at the end of the calendar month if possible. When you close closer to the beginning of the month, you will have to pay the interest on the loan for the rest of the month along with the down payment. If you close at the end of the month, the interest will be figured in with the rest of your payments.

Remember, while it may seem as if you're locked into a loan that will last forever, homeowners can refinance their homes to get a better interest rate. If interest rates should drop by several percentage points during the course of your mortgage, it may be worthwhile to refinance your home at a lower rate.

MOVING IN

Now that you have chosen your new home, you are ready to move in. You can either move yourself or have someone else move your possessions for you. What you decide will depend on your needs. If you hire a moving company, you can save money by packing your possessions yourself (although you should be aware that anything you pack may not be insured if it isn't packed well). Depending on how far away from your destination you are, you may want to rent a truck or van, or even use pickup trucks. Friends and relatives will usually be agreeable to helping you move, especially when they know you will return the favor. Of course, moving can be a bit traumatic, but with friends around—and with the proper preparation and tips like those that follow—it can actually be fun.

Stock up on sturdy and manageable boxes. Liquor stores are an excellent source of free heavy-duty boxes. We raised some eyebrows when we moved the first time. Our neighbors knew we didn't have wild parties, yet we were filling our car to the top with beer boxes. We chose them because they were small enough to fit almost anywhere and they were easy to lift.

Don't pack things like jewelry and immediate-need items with your other possessions. Medicines and toiletries should be hand-carried, since you don't want to have to dig through all those boxes right away when you get to your destination.

Label your boxes. Either write the contents on each box or number the boxes and keep track of what is in each one on a separate sheet of paper. Write on each box in big letters the name of the room into which it goes. If you're working with a professional mover, make sure everything is listed on their manifest before you sign it. If it's not, you have no course of action if something is lost.

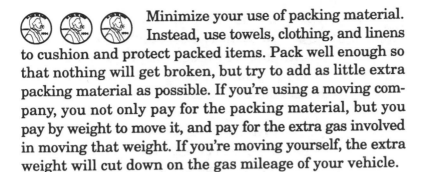 Minimize your use of packing material. Instead, use towels, clothing, and linens to cushion and protect packed items. Pack well enough so that nothing will get broken, but try to add as little extra packing material as possible. If you're using a moving company, you not only pay for the packing material, but you pay by weight to move it, and pay for the extra gas involved in moving that weight. If you're moving yourself, the extra weight will cut down on the gas mileage of your vehicle.

PROTECTING YOUR INVESTMENT

One of the very first things you should do when you move into a new home is to arrange for the appropriate amount of protection to insure your property against fire, theft, and other types of loss. If you rent, you should have enough insurance to protect your personal possessions—your clothes, appliances, furniture, dishes, etc. When you purchase a home, however, you must have insurance to protect both your and the mortgageholder's investment, so insurance is *required* before you can buy the house. Make sure that you have enough insurance to cover the replacement value of your possessions and your home at the current price, which means that your policy should take inflation into consideration. If you make any major improvements or additions to the house, get in touch with your insurance agent to have your insurance adjusted accordingly. This way, if the value of your house goes up, and if you should suffer a loss, your insurance will be adequate to pay for rebuilding or buying a comparable home. Although insurance can be a major expense, there are some ways to cut down on the cost. Many are simple safety measures that reduce risks and therefore the insurance premiums.

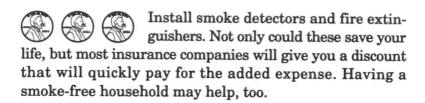 Install smoke detectors and fire extin-
guishers. Not only could these save your
life, but most insurance companies will give you a discount
that will quickly pay for the added expense. Having a
smoke-free household may help, too.

Install a security system and use dead-
bolt locks on all outside doors. Outside
doors with windows located near the doorknob should be
replaced. Use a heavy rod in the track of sliding glass doors
and windows to prevent them from sliding open. Keep your
property well lit. Most companies charge less to insure
secure homes.

When you're away from home, take care
not to "advertise" that your home is
empty. Hook your lights up to automatic timers and have
mail and newspaper delivery stopped, or have a friend pick
them up for you. Ask a friend or a neighbor to park his or
her car in your driveway, and to cut your grass if necessary before you return.

Make friends with your neighbors. The
neighborhood watch system is based on
the idea that more eyes watching can cut down on the success rate of criminals. If you get to know your neighbors,
you can notice if a stranger is at their house when they're
not home. Your neighbors can return the favor.

FURNISHINGS AND APPLIANCES

Now that you have your house you'll want to furnish it.
You may not be able to afford new things right away, so
shop around. And keep in mind that you don't have to fur-

nish the entire house in the first month, or even in the first year; many people take years to complete the furnishing process, as their budget allows. Until you can save some money and budget for new furnishings, keep the following suggestions in mind.

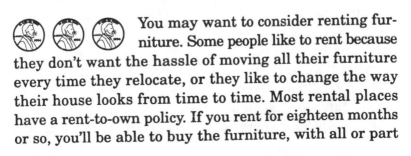 Prioritize your furnishings list. Decide what is absolutely necessary immediately and what can wait until the budget is more forgiving. A refrigerator and cooking stove are essential; fancy tables, expensive curtains, and attractive lamps can wait.

Check out thrift stores like the Salvation Army or Goodwill Industries for used or damaged furniture at reasonable prices. Church thrift stores, garage sales, and estate sales are also good sources of used furniture. Department stores often sell at a discount furniture that has been slightly damaged, reconditioned, or repossessed. You may want to ask at your local Sears, Wards, or Penney's to see if they have a showroom for this type of furniture. Sometimes stores consolidate discounted appliances and furniture at a single store or even a separate location. Look for manufacturers' or furniture-store outlet shops as well. Also, try a rental clearance center for used rental furniture that is in good condition.

You may want to consider renting furniture. Some people like to rent because they don't want the hassle of moving all their furniture every time they relocate, or they like to change the way their house looks from time to time. Most rental places have a rent-to-own policy. If you rent for eighteen months or so, you'll be able to buy the furniture, with all or part of your rental payments credited towards the purchase. Before choosing this option, however, check how much the total price of renting would be compared to buying the same item directly from a store. It may cost you more when you apply your rental towards ownership.

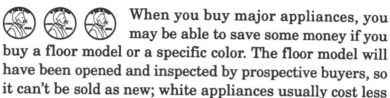 When you buy major appliances, you may be able to save some money if you buy a floor model or a specific color. The floor model will have been opened and inspected by prospective buyers, so it can't be sold as new; white appliances usually cost less than other colors.

HOME MAINTENANCE

When you were renting, if something around the house needed repairing, you probably called the realtor, the superintendent, or the landlord. As a homeowner, you will not have the luxury of calling someone every time a repair is needed. Indeed, you'll quickly discover the truth in the old saying that "there's always something to do around the house," and you'll have the dilemma of trying to fix the problem yourself or paying an arm and a leg to a professional. Often preventive maintenance—simple things like cleaning filters, vacuuming coils, and oiling moving parts—will extend the life of an appliance or another part of your home for years. For instance, turn off the water to your washing machine between washes to reduce the stress on hoses and valves that can lead to their breaking, perhaps flooding your washroom. Vacuuming the coils of your refrigerator will allow it to operate more efficiently, thus using less electricity and leading to a longer life for the refrigerator. Likewise, changing the air filters on your furnace monthly will save energy and repairs. Disposing of grease from cooking by pouring it into a can or jar and putting it in the garbage (instead of pouring it down the drain) will end up saving you money in plumbers' fees. Maintaining your property, home, and furnishings will extend their life and minimize the need for repairs, saving you money.

Repairs

Even with the best attention to maintenance, however, the need for repairs around the house is a fact of life. You can save a lot of money if you can handle at least some of these problems on your own. There are many home repair manuals on the market now that even I can understand, and a good one could easily save you its purchase price the first time your plumbing breaks down. When faced with the need for home repair, keep the following points in mind.

Learn how to perform simple repairs *before* the need arises. For example, you should learn how to relight pilot lights on everything in your house that runs on gas *before* you have to do it in the dark or while standing half-clothed and freezing. A common problem with gas stoves is the clogging of a burner by carbon deposits. If this happens, turn on one of the other burners to see where the flames are supposed to be coming through. Clean those areas on the inoperative burner with a pipe cleaner. Since pipe cleaners have a wire core, they can get into small holes.

Caution: Do not attempt any other repairs on gas-related items unless you have been trained to do this type of repair work. Natural gas is explosive and very dangerous; if you haven't been properly trained, you could end up causing a gas leak and possibly property damage and bodily injury.

As soon as you move into your new home, learn how to locate the power box and replace a fuse or reset a tripped circuit breaker. Since darkness and tripped breakers tend to go together, it's a good idea to stash a flashlight nearby where you can get your hands on it by feel. If you're doing any electrical work, flip off the circuit breaker or remove the fuse for the area you're working in. Better still, be on the safe side and cut off all power that is not needed to get the work done.

If you are faced with a repair job that is beyond your talents, then call a qualified technician. Find out the precise terms beforehand. Some businesses will give you a free estimate; others will charge you for the estimate and apply that charge towards your bill if you choose them do the job. Try to set up your appointment for early in the day, if possible. After a certain hour, you may have to pay time and a half. We had a leaking faucet that was beyond our talent, so we called a repairman and an appointment was made. Just before the repairman was due to arrive, his dispatcher called and said he would be an hour late. He finally arrived three hours later, as I was on my way out to work. When my husband was presented with the bill, he nearly went into shock. The price was not what we had been quoted on the phone. Because the repairman arrived just after 6:00 P.M., the work he did was considered "overtime" and we were charged 50 percent more than the standard rate for his labor. Always double-check that the price is going to be the same as was verbally agreed.

   If you're planning a major home repair or improvement like a new roof, siding, central air conditioning, or the addition of a new room, you may be forced to take out another loan. A construction company may ask you to sign a lien on your property, which means that if you miss a few payments to this creditor you could lose your house. If the improvement is not absolutely necessary, you would be better off to wait until you can save at least part of the money for it in advance. You could also consider a home equity loan (see Chapter 2, Managing Your Money).

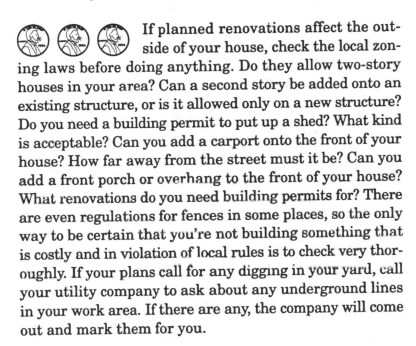 If planned renovations affect the outside of your house, check the local zoning laws before doing anything. Do they allow two-story houses in your area? Can a second story be added onto an existing structure, or is it allowed only on a new structure? Do you need a building permit to put up a shed? What kind is acceptable? Can you add a carport onto the front of your house? How far away from the street must it be? Can you add a front porch or overhang to the front of your house? What renovations do you need building permits for? There are even regulations for fences in some places, so the only way to be certain that you're not building something that is costly and in violation of local rules is to check very thoroughly. If your plans call for any digging in your yard, call your utility company to ask about any underground lines in your work area. If there are any, the company will come out and mark them for you.

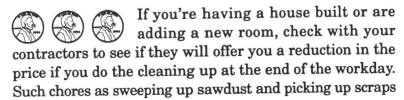 If you're having a house built or are adding a new room, check with your contractors to see if they will offer you a reduction in the price if you do the cleaning up at the end of the workday. Such chores as sweeping up sawdust and picking up scraps

of wood are necessary for safety, and this takes time—time you're paying the contractor for. Depending on the size of the project, a deal like this could save you several hundred dollars.

Housework

The old adage says that only two things in life are certain: death and taxes. Obviously the person who said this never had to do housework. Whether you're single or married, a man or woman, if you have a home, you will have to do housework of one kind or another.

One time-consuming chore that can involve a big expense is cleaning. There are shelves upon shelves in the supermarket filled with expensive cleaning products. But if you heed the following suggestions you will find that there are ample opportunities to pinch pennies here as well.

Limit the number of different cleaning preparations you use. Advertisers tell us we need a different cleaner for each job, but actually you can keep your home just as clean with two inexpensive chemicals: ammonia and bleach. Buy the generic brands, and use them to clean almost everything. Both will kill most bacteria and other microbes. Use bleach to whiten your clothes, of course, but also to kill mildew in the bath, washroom, or anywhere else it occurs. Pour bleach down your drains twice a month to keep them unclogged; it works faster and is cheaper than commercial drain cleaners. Ammonia makes an excellent glass cleaner, and it can be used to clean counters, stoves, the inside and outside of refrigerators, floors, and just about anything else.

Caution: Follow the dilution directions on the labels, and *don't* mix ammonia and bleach together. Also, when using bleach, be sure to wear rubber gloves and old clothing; bleach can splash and permanently discolor any fabric it touches.

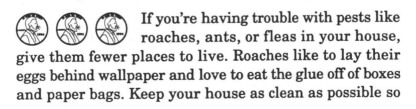 If you're a little low on cash and you need other cleaning supplies, use other household items to replace specialty cleaning products. Shampoo will remove ring around the collar. Vinegar or lemon juice will cut grease, and both are good glass cleaners. When added to hot water, they can cut through grease in your drains and pipes; frozen into ice cubes, they can be run through the garbage disposal to clean it. Baking soda makes an excellent scouring powder. Use crumpled newspapers to dry off windows or mirrors. In addition to saving money, this cuts down on streaking. Hair spray or styling mist will get out most ballpoint ink marks on clothing. Hydrogen peroxide works well on blood stains and other organic stains. If little Johnny gets chewing gum on his clothes, apply a little peanut butter to the gum, then scrape the gum off. Treat the soiled spot with shampoo.

Keep your use of paper towels to a minimum. For most household cleaning, use cellulose sponges or cloth rags (a great way to recycle old clothing and towels that have passed beyond the point of repair), which can be washed and used again and again. In the kitchen, keep a terry-cloth towel close to the sink to be used for drying hands only (not dishes).

If you're having trouble with pests like roaches, ants, or fleas in your house, give them fewer places to live. Roaches like to lay their eggs behind wallpaper and love to eat the glue off of boxes and paper bags. Keep your house as clean as possible so roaches won't have a feast every night after the lights go out. Vacuum the coils on your refrigerator and the tops of drapes. These are warm places that often go unnoticed. Also, clean out under and behind cabinets, and anywhere else that pests might live, at regular intervals. In general, you can cut off most pests' sources of food by investing in containers with airtight seals. Professional exterminators are expensive and should be called only as a last resort—you have better things to do with your money.

Look for organic or sound ecological alternatives for pest control. Boric acid is the main ingredient in most of those expensive concoctions for controlling roaches, for example. (Remember, however, to store it where children and pets cannot reach it, as it can be poisonous if ingested.) Bug sprays should be used only as a last resort because even though they kill bugs, they are costly and they irritate humans (and pets) in the process. Some pests dislike different spices or cleaning agents. Mice dislike the smell of peppermint; ants don't like cloves or red pepper; fleas will flee from salt water. Putting fresh bay leaves in your cupboards will keep many pests away for up to a year.

If outdoor pests are bugging your garden, use natural methods—which cost less and won't harm the environment—to help your plants flourish. The best method to control many attached or slow-moving insects, for example, is to pick the offenders off your plants by hand (carry a small jar of water to drown them in) or wash them off with a hose. If you have slugs or snails in your yard, sink a pie pan or the lid of a jar into the ground and fill it with beer so that the beer is at ground level. These creatures will be attracted to the beer, fall in, and dissolve. You can also try cultivating beneficial insects, such as ladybugs and praying mantises, which will eat a variety of pests. When you plan your garden, remember that certain plants will repel insects. Marigolds, which are very easy to grow from seed and therefore inexpensive, are often planted around the edges of vegetable gardens for this purpose. Planting radishes near green beans can help discourage bean beetles. Investigate what plants might help control the particular pests that are causing your problems, and plan accordingly.

One area few people bother to look for savings is in the garbage. Unless you have municipal garbage collection, you probably just routinely pay the trash collection bill (usually after grumbling a little about how high the rates are getting). The reason the rates are getting higher is that space in landfills is getting scarcer. This is why, in many areas, if you exceed a certain limited allowance, you are charged for the collection of each additional garbage can or bag. The solution: Get into recycling. Learn to sort out your recyclables—metals, glass, cardboard, paper, plastics, batteries, and other items— and either put them out for curbside recycling (if it's available in your area) or bring them to a recycling center. If possible, look for places that will pay you for your recyclables. Return any deposit bottles and cans. You can dramatically decrease the amount of garbage you throw away by first removing the recyclable material. If you're lucky, instead of paying someone to haul your garbage away, you'll be getting paid for it—and you'll be helping the environment at the same time.

Maintaining a home takes time and effort, but it's well worth it. Likewise, buying and living in your own home presents certain challenges and potential difficulties, but there are sound financial reasons why home ownership makes sense. Be prepared to take advantage of these penny-pinching (indeed, dollar-saving) opportunities if they can work for you. One of the greatest joys in life, for most people, comes with the satisfaction of owning their own special place—to clean, maintain, decorate, and fret over—and it's nice to know that something that can add so much quality to your life can save you money, too!

6

Saving Energy

Energy conservation has become a major concern in the United States; we're all beginning to realize that the world's fossil fuel resources aren't infinite. The more we deplete these resources, the more expensive the remaining fuels become. It's just common sense to limit our use of energy—both to save our resources and to save money.

Each year, people in the United States pay almost $100 billion for the use of energy for heating and cooling their homes, for cooking and refrigeration, for lighting, and for other "necessary" conveniences like water heaters, dishwashers, stereos, televisions, and computers. There are many simple steps you can take to save energy in your home and reduce the size of your bills, usually with little or no discomfort to you or your family. For the most part, measures to save energy merely involve increasing your Energy Quotient or EQ—learning a few basic principles and using your common sense—but like all the other penny-pinching ideas I've been describing, they frequently require you to plan ahead and be judicious in your use of time and money. If you are willing to take the time, you can put some savings into your bank account and help our country's energy situation at the same time.

If you're building or seeking to purchase a home, investigate its energy status thoroughly while you still have an opportunity to change it without major expense. If you're building, make energy considerations a top priority, and take a personal interest in the kind and size of the heating and/or air conditioning system, the insulation, the doors and windows, and the natural surroundings. If you're buying, consider the same factors, but in addition, ask to see previous utility bills. You may want to consult an expert who can advise you about the energy efficiency of the house. Some utility companies offer to perform free "home energy audits" as well.

When you're buying a new major appliance, check the energy efficiency ratio (EER) sticker. The higher the EER, the more efficient the product is. For air conditioners, the range is from 10 to 15, with the lowest rated using 50 percent more energy than the highest. Even though the EER is an average number, you can use it to estimate what it will cost you per year to use an appliance if you know how much energy costs per unit in your region of the country and about how many hours per year you're likely to use it. For central heating systems, energy efficiency is measured in Average Fuel Utilization Efficiency units (AFUE). A good system will have a rating of 85 to 95 AFUE, meaning that it is 85- to 95-percent efficient.

Check to see if your local utility company has any incentive programs for conserving energy during peak hours. Often you can receive a credit on your electric bill simply by allowing the company the right to control your power during periods of peak usage. Consumers use the most energy at certain times of the day, called peak hours. The change in season often dictates a change in energy usage. In summer, the peak hours are late afternoon and early evening; this is usually the hottest part of the day, when air conditioners are being run at full blast and when meals are being cooked, dishes washed, etc. In winter, the peak hours are later, during the coldest and darkest part of the day when people are awake.

Avoid using heat-producing appliances as much as possible, particularly in summer, and time their usage to coincide with the coolest part of the day. In summer, cook your meals when it's cool and reheat the food in your microwave later, or serve meals that need minimal cooking. Barbecuing is also a good alternative because the heat produced by cooking is outdoors instead of being trapped inside your house. Do other energy-consuming chores as early in the morning as possible to avoid causing a big energy drain when the air conditioner is on.

Utility companies often have programs to help consumers become more energy efficient—and therefore save money. One area we lived in had a Zero Interest Program, in which the utility company would lend money interest-free to consumers so that they could add specific energy-saving products to their homes. Some utility companies offer rebates if you buy energy-efficient appliances. Many companies also offer the option of averaging your utility bill out over the year. While this program doesn't necessarily save you money, it prevents you from being hit with a big bill at any one time, which in turn allows you to plan your budget and use your money more wisely.

Each of the sections that follow should help you improve your EQ. Hopefully you will build on this information and adapt it to your unique situation.

HEATING AND COOLING

If you're like most Americans, by far the largest part (over 46 percent) of your residential energy use will go for the heating and cooling of your home. Regardless of what kind of home you live in, and regardless of the type of heating and cooling system you have, you probably can make significant reductions in the amount of energy you are using almost immediately. Consider the following suggestions.

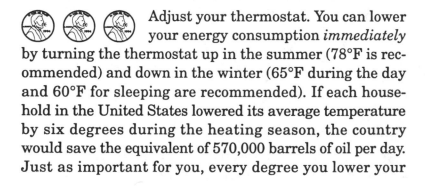 Dress wisely. The human body is a type of combustion chamber, or heater, giving off some 350 British thermal units (BTUs) of heat an hour. In winter, instead of allowing this heat to dissipate into the surrounding atmosphere, wouldn't it make sense to trap more of the heat closer to your body to make you feel warmer? Wearing several layers of clothes instead of one heavy piece can equal as much as five or more degrees in warmth. So instead of wearing one heavy sweater, wear a sweatshirt over another shirt, and then add a lighter sweater. The layers of air between the layers of clothing act as added insulation to retain more of your body's natural heat. In my parents' home, we used the lovely afghans my grandmothers made to keep ourselves warm while sitting in the living room and watching television. Conversely, in the summer, wear as little clothing as necessary, and keep what you do wear lightweight and loose.

Adjust your thermostat. You can lower your energy consumption *immediately* by turning the thermostat up in the summer (78°F is recommended) and down in the winter (65°F during the day and 60°F for sleeping are recommended). If each household in the United States lowered its average temperature by six degrees during the heating season, the country would save the equivalent of 570,000 barrels of oil per day. Just as important for you, every degree you lower your thermostat in the winter or raise it in the summer will save dollars on your energy bill *and* extend the life of your heating or cooling system. And if you're dressing sensibly, you'll hardly feel the difference.

Test your house for airtightness. Feel around windows, doors, and cracks to discover air leaks. You should also check around pipes, electrical wires and outlets, ceiling fixtures, and foldaway stairs to the attic. Caulk or weatherstrip anyplace that leaks air. Weatherstripping, which is sold in strips or on rolls like tape, is used to fill any gaps around doors or windows. Caulking is like weatherstripping, except it's used to fill gaps where weatherstripping isn't a practical option. You can fill in gaps that occur around pipes, between boards on a wall, or around the outside edges of window frames. Caulk will expand, so don't cram it into cracks. Use a little bit less than you think you need. Caulking and weatherstripping, if you do the work yourself, costs about fifty dollars for the average house, and might save you as much as 10 percent on your energy bill.

Install double-pane glass, or storm doors and windows. Double-glazed (thermal) windows and storm windows are similar. They both have an extra layer of glass with an air space, which adds extra insulation, between them. Storm windows are installed over regular windows and can be taken down, while double-glazed or thermal windows are permanent. Triple-glazing is also an option for extremely cold areas. If you can't afford any of these, seal your windows with plastic film to cut down heat loss, which you can do yourself for about ten dollars. The plastic film adheres to the window frame to form a good seal. Another type of plastic can be stretched over the window and shrunk to fit with the heat of a normal hair dryer.

I had a friend when I was in the military whose dormitory room was very cold in the winter, and there was very little she could do about it. She got a large, corrugated cardboard appliance box and cut it into panels that fit into her windows for use while she slept. This made enough of a difference in the room temperature to make it livable. This idea is practical for renters because it is energy efficient without altering the property, and the materials cost almost nothing. The panels can be decorated with paint or contact paper for a dressier appearance.

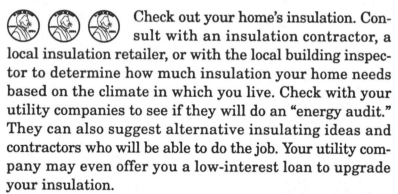 Check out your home's insulation. Consult with an insulation contractor, a local insulation retailer, or with the local building inspector to determine how much insulation your home needs based on the climate in which you live. Check with your utility companies to see if they will do an "energy audit." They can also suggest alternative insulating ideas and contractors who will be able to do the job. Your utility company may even offer you a low-interest loan to upgrade your insulation.

Every home needs insulation, no matter what your climate's like, and in most environments you should have adequate insulation in the ceiling or attic, under the floor, and in the walls. Ask and learn about R-values. These are numbers used to rate the effectiveness of insulation material. To get an idea of the amount of insulation your home should have, see How Much Insulation Do You Need? on page 128.

If you do install new or additional insulation, make sure

it is mounted properly, with the vapor barrier (the paper or foil layer) facing towards the heat source in your home, to avoid moisture problems. Although insulation is expensive when you buy it, it can save you as much as 30 percent per year on your heating and cooling bills, so it pays for itself very quickly.

Keep your heating and air conditioning equipment running efficiently. Have the burners and other working parts checked by a professional periodically, always in the off season when the rates are lower. You can check to see that all ducts are not leaking and are wrapped in insulation, and that filters are clean.

If you have a gas furnace with a pilot light, find out how much it would cost to convert to electronic ignition, which for a typical home costs about fifty dollars less a year to operate. If your house has electric heat, you might consider converting to gas or to a heat pump, which "pumps" heat from the air into your house and could save you about 30 percent on your electric bill.

If you don't have an air conditioning or central heating unit, but are thinking of getting one, keep in mind the energy efficiency ratio, which ranks a unit according to the amount of energy used and its cost to you. Buy a heating or cooling system that fits your house. If you're planning on adding a room onto your house, make allowance for the extra space. A system that's too small will be running all the time, and a system that's too big is a waste of your money.

How Much Insulation
Do You Need?

All homes need some insulation. But how much you need depends on where you live. Also, different areas of your home should have different amounts. The ceilings of top floors, for example, need more insulation than floors over the basement do, because more heat is lost and gained through the ceiling. The climate you live in, the type of heating system you have (houses that heat with electricity generally should have better insulation), and the kind of insulation material you choose will all affect the amount of insulation you need.

The first step in determining your insulation needs is to find out which heating / insulation zone you live in (see Figure 6.1). Then you can figure out how effective the insulation in different areas of your home should be. The effectiveness of insulation is measured in R-values, which represent the resistance of insulation materials to either gaining or losing heat. The higher the R-value number, the higher the degree of insulation.

Four key places to insulate are exterior walls; crawlspace walls; floors over unheated crawlspaces and basements; and ceilings below ventilated attics. In exterior walls, most houses should have insulation rated at R-11, regardless of where they are located or what type of heating system they have. In crawlspace walls, houses in zone 1 should have R-11, and those in all other zones should have R-19. In floors that are over unheated crawlspaces and basements, no insulation is necessary if you live in zone 1 or 2; if you live in zone 3 and have electric heat, you should have R-19, as you should in all other zones (regardless of the type of heating system). The amount of insulation needed in ceilings below attics varies the most. In zone 1, you should have R-19 (R-30 if you have electric heat); in zone 2, you will need R-30; in zones 3 and 4, R-30 (R-38 if you have electric heat); in zones 5 and 6, R-38; in zone 7, R-38 (R-49 if you have electric heat); and in zone 8, R-49.

Once you know the recommended R-values, you can figure out how much insulation you will need to achieve them. This depends on the type of insulation you choose. The most commonly used types of insulation materials fall into two basic categories: blanket or batts (either mineral fiber or fiberglass), and loose and blown fill, such as cellulosic fiber. Generally, mineral fiber and loose and blown fill will give you similar R-values for the thickness. Fiberglass insulation will have to be slightly thicker to have the same effect. Other types of insulation include rigid cellular insulating boards, rock-wool, perlite, and vermiculite. Whichever product you use, always consult the manufacturer's recommendation for the thickness required to achieve the R-value you need and for proper application.

Figure 6.1 Heating/Insullation Zone Map

The amount of insulation you need in different places in your home depends on the climate you live in, the type of heating system you have, and the type of insulation you

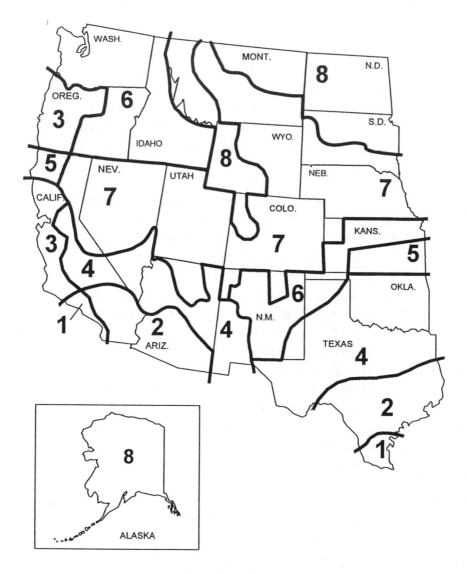

use. The map below divides the United States into eight heating/insulation zones that correspond to general climatic conditions.

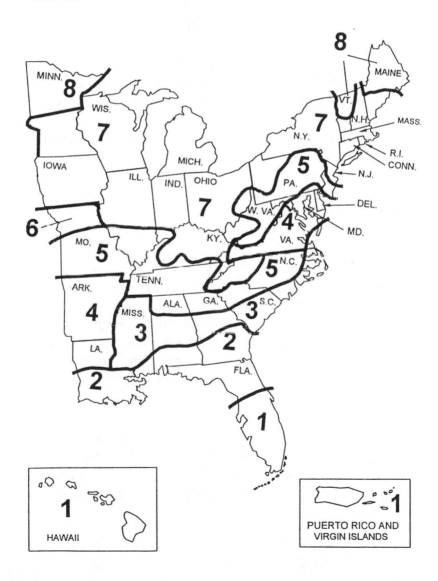

If you have a fireplace, use it sparingly. Fireplaces are pretty and create a romantic or cozy atmosphere, but they are terribly inefficient as heaters. The heat from a fireplace is mostly confined to the room in which the fireplace is located, and heat from the rest of the house tends to move into that room and flow up the open chimney. Keep the damper in the chimney closed when the fireplace is not in use; otherwise, the chimney will suck warm air out of your house. When you do light a fire in the fireplace, close off the remainder of the house if possible. If isolating the fireplace is not a viable option, then lower the thermostat so the other heat source will not run unnecessarily. If you must depend on a fireplace for heat, consider adding an insert, a convective grate, or at least a glass screen to reduce wasted heat and therefore wasted money. Be aware, however, that a fireplace insert stays very hot for a long time after a fire goes out. If you have small children, you'll want to find some way to protect them from burning themselves.

If you burn wood, instead of trashing or recycling your newspapers, collect them in the summer months and roll them into tight logs. For the best results, wet the papers before you roll them up. The water will make the paper stick together to burn more like a log. Set your logs aside to dry thoroughly, and you'll appreciate the news again in the winter as you're sitting in front of a cozy fire.

Check to see where the thermostat is located in your house. If it's on an outside wall or near a window, it may not be as accurate as it would be if it were on a wall away from windows. Set your thermostat as high (summer) and as low (winter) as is comfortable for the circumstances. In the summer, for example, you might wear loose-fitting shirts and shorts most of the time, but if company is coming, you might plan to run the air conditioner more to cool down the house. Also, consider buying a timer for your thermostat; it may cost fifty dollars or so, but unless you are careful to turn your thermostat up or down every night, and when you leave the house for several hours at a time, you are wasting energy to heat and cool an empty (or sleeping) home. In time, your energy savings will pay for the timer.

Use fans instead of air conditioning as much as possible. Fans use a lot less energy than an air conditioner, and they are usually a lot quieter and perhaps even healthier for you and your family. Ceiling fans are easy to install and can be used to circulate air in the winter as well as in the summer. In the summertime, a ceiling fan can make as much as a six-degree difference in comfortable temperature (air moving past your skin has a cooling effect even if the air is warm). Many ceiling fans are also reversible, making them useful in the wintertime also for better heat distribution. Even better, install a whole-house fan in your attic or upstairs window. Except for the hottest, most humid days of the year, when the temperature doesn't drop much at night, you can use the whole-house fan in place of air conditioning. The fan pulls air in through the windows, cooling you, and then forces the warmer air out through the attic.

If you have a central air-conditioning unit that sits on the ground, make sure to keep weeds and grass cut away from it. Grass and weeds can block its airway and decrease its efficiency. Window-mounted air conditioners need some air space, too. If possible, an air-conditioning unit should be mounted where it gets the least amount of direct sunlight, or you can plant trees and shrubs at a slight distance where they will block sunlight off as they grow. Air conditioners operate about 10 percent more efficiently in the shade.

Consider buying insulated curtains and shades, which work like insulation to reduce the unwanted flow of heat either into or out of your house. Although not insulated, Venetian blinds, regular shades, and mini-blinds can help also. Shade screens cut down on summertime heat, too. These can't be adjusted to block out all the light, like blinds or shades, but they do reduce it somewhat.

Learn to use sunshine and nature's own heating/cooling system to your advantage—you'll be surprised how much energy you can save and still be comfortable! In many parts of the United States, nights are cool at least nine or ten months of the year. If you're trying to keep the house cool, open the windows at night and allow cool air to flow in (a whole-house fan allows you to dramatically increase the air flow). In the morning, when the sun begins to heat up the outside air, close the windows and curtains on the side of the house that is hit by direct sun. You can keep the windows on the "dark side" of the house open for air circulation if necessary. On the other hand, if it's cold outside and you want to keep the house warm, keep the windows shut. Keep your curtains, blinds, or shades shut until the sun comes out, and then open the curtains (especially on the sunny side) to let the sun warm up (and light up!) the house. When the sun goes down, close the curtains again to keep in the warmth.

 Install roof vents or roof turbines to help with temperature regulation in the summer. If it's extremely hot, your attic will heat up like an oven. No matter how high the R-value of your insulation, the heat will eventually soak through to your living space if you haven't provided a way for it to escape. Roof vents and turbines will provide an escape route for the excess heat. (Turbines must be sealed off in the winter to prevent heat loss.)

If you have a gas furnace with a pilot light, turn it off in the summer.
Caution: Be certain you know how to relight the pilot before turning on the furnace in the fall; otherwise, you might be pinching pennies in heaven.

THE KITCHEN

Next to the heating and cooling systems of your home, the appliances in your kitchen are the second biggest energy consumers. Like your heating system, the refrigerator runs continuously; your stove and dishwasher, like all other appliances that generate or remove heat, use a substantial amount of electricity. Your kitchen offers plenty of opportunities for increasing efficiency, reducing energy consumption—and pinching pennies.

Refrigeration

About 15 percent of all the energy you use goes to your refrigerator/freezer, so any steps you can take to control the cost of operating this appliance can save you lots of money. Keep the following points in mind to cool down the cost of running your refrigerator.

Don't keep the refrigerator or freezer colder than necessary (38°F to 40°F is recommended for the refrigerator, 5°F for the freezer section), and make sure the doors fit tightly. You can check the seals by closing each door on a five-dollar bill, which is about how much extra your refrigerator is costing you every three months if the seal isn't tight. If the bill slides out, or if you can pull it out easily, then you need to adjust the hinges or replace the seal.

Don't open and shut the refrigerator all the time. Every time you open the refrigerator door, you suck out the cold air. This means the refrigerator has to cool down all over again. In the summer, I cut down on the opening and closing by keeping a jug of ice water on the kitchen counter. I fill a cooler jug with ice and water in the morning, and as the day progresses, the ice melts and the water stays cold. If you are buying a new refrigerator, consider one that gives you access to ice and water outside the door. In general, think about what you want before you open your refrigerator or freezer and try to pull out everything you need at one time.

Don't pack your freezer absolutely full, but don't leave it empty, either. There has to be enough room for the cold air to circulate, but remember, mass stores cold, so if there's not much food in your freezer the compressor will run overtime to keep it cold. If you let the freezer become nearly empty between shopping trips, you might want to stuff it with newspapers or with trays of water to freeze. Take your frozen foods out of the plastic or paper bags they were put in for the trip home from the store; they will freeze faster if they're in smaller packages and scattered around the freezer.

Avoid putting hot food in your refrigerator or freezer. The food will raise the internal temperature of your appliance and force it to work harder to get cool again. The warmer temperature also gives bacteria and molds a better chance to grow on your foods.

If possible, locate your refrigerator away from your dishwasher or oven. Both the dishwasher and the oven radiate heat, causing the refrigerator to work harder to stay cool. If your refrigerator must be near one of these appliances, put some sort of insulation between them.

If your refrigerator does not have automatic defrosting, defrost it regularly. The more frost that accumulates, the harder the freezer has to work. Never let frost build up more than one-quarter inch thick. Clean the coils on your refrigerator at least once a year; dirty coils can prevent your icemaker from working properly also.

Cooking and Dishwashing

Another big energy consumer is the stove. This is why you should always use the smallest appliance possible (a pressure cooker, crockpot, toaster oven, deep fryer, microwave) to cook a given quantity of food. However, since you must use the stove for some cooking, always keep the burners, reflectors, and oven clean to assure maximum efficiency.

If you have a gas stove, make sure the pilot is burning with a blue flame—which indicates efficient combustion. If you plan to purchase a gas unit, find one with an electronic ignition system instead of a pilot light—you'll use about one-third less gas.

Whatever type of stove you have, remember to match the size of the pot or pan to the size of the heating element or flame, and always cook with low to moderate heat. The higher the flame or setting, the more energy you use and the more chance you have of burning the contents. You can cut down on cooking time by putting a lid on your pan. (Make sure the lid is on a little bit crooked, so that there is a crack for steam to escape. Otherwise, you may end up having your meal boil over onto the stove.) With an electric range, practice the trick of turning off the burner a few minutes before the allotted cooking time ends—the heating element will remain hot long enough to complete the cooking without electricity.

I certainly don't recommend using your oven to heat your kitchen, but in winter it can do double duty. Since I'm from Minnesota, I learned my mom's secret for heating the house on a cold winter morning. She did her baking in the morning so the heat from the oven would warm up the house, and she could keep the thermostat set to a lower temperature. Remember, though, the oven is designed to keep heat in, not to heat the house. Always use a timer rather than continually opening the oven door when baking.

Because your oven isn't very efficient, you should use it as infrequently as you can, but when you do heat it up, try to bake as much as possible at one time. For example, you can prepare several dishes that can be refrigerated or frozen for later consumption. You also might plan meals that allow you to bake your bread, meat, and vegetables simultaneously (not for the same amount of time, of course). If you leave the oven door shut, the oven should hold enough heat to continue baking for ten minutes after you turn it off. This can save energy—and money—if you're making a long-cooking dish.

When you have just a few dishes to wash, or if you have enough time to do the job, you should wash dishes by hand and save the extra water and energy required by a dishwasher. Instead of running water constantly, run water to rinse only after all the dishes have been soaped. If you use a dishwasher, wash full loads only and make sure the dishes are well scraped and rinsed in cold water first. The typical dishwasher uses about fifteen gallons of hot water per load, so you are paying dearly for the convenience. Always utilize the most economical setting, and allow the dishes to air dry after the final rinse (open the dishwasher door).

THE LAUNDRY AND WATER USE

You can save money by doing your own laundry, but here again you should take pains to plan your washing routine to take full advantage of energy savings. For example, if you can do most of your washing on sunny days, and if you have a yard or an area big enough to put up a clothesline, you can save considerable energy by drying your clothes outdoors. If you don't like to hang your clothes on the line because they get stiff, put them in the dryer for about five minutes to soften them up before hanging them out. They'll be less wrinkled this way, too, and clothes dried in the sunshine smell cleaner and fresher.

Many people can't always hang their clothes outside to dry. Your next best alternative is to maintain your washer and dryer at peak efficiency by keeping filters, hoses, and exhausts clean and unobstructed. You can save energy with your washer by washing only full loads, in either cold or warm water, and by always rinsing in cold water. Don't use too much detergent, which can cause your machine to work harder and use more energy. Cut down on your drying time with a heavier wash by putting it through an extra spin cycle in the washer. The dryer uses more than twice as much energy as the washer because energy is needed for the heating element as well as for the motor. If you reduce the amount of water in the clothes while they're in the washer, you don't have to use the dryer as long.

Try to wash and dry clothes in consecutive loads. Much of the initial energy a dryer consumes goes to heat the dryer itself; once it is heated up, you should keep it hot and working to dry clothes more efficiently.

One appliance that I haven't mentioned yet is central to most of what you do around the house—your hot water heater. Heating water takes about 15 percent of the energy used in the home. You can save energy (and money!) by heating your water more efficiently. By insulating your water heater and water pipes, fixing leaky faucets, and setting your water heater to a lower temperature, you can save several dollars each month. Insulating your water heater and the water pipes allows less heat to escape, thus reducing the amount of energy needed to regulate the water temperature. A temperature setting of 120°F provides adequate hot water for most situations, and besides saving energy, this also prevents serious accidental burning from the water being too hot. At 120°F, water takes three minutes to cause a third-degree burn; at 140°F, it can cause a third-degree burn in as little as *five seconds*, which may not be long enough for you to get yourself—or a young child—out of harm's way. And by reducing the temperature setting from 140°F to 120°F, you should save about 18 percent of the energy used for heating water. Also, drain some water from the bottom faucet of your heater every few months to release some of the sediment buildup. The thicker the buildup of sediment, the more energy is being wasted in heating the water.

In addition to lowering the temperature of your hot water, you should look for ways to reduce the amount of hot water you use. Using less hot water to wash clothes and dishes helps, and you can learn to use less to keep yourself clean, too! Take short, efficient showers. A normal tub bath requires about thirty gallons of water, whereas a typical shower of five minutes uses only about fifteen gallons. In addition, you can easily install water-saver shower heads, which can restrict the flow of water to three gallons of water per minute or less—but still provide adequate water for a comfortable shower. When you're running water for a bath, start the hot water first, then add cold water to achieve a comfortable temperature. Cooling down hot water takes less energy than trying to warm up cold water.

Another major user of water in your home is the toilet, and older toilets especially can be real water-wasters. A simple, inexpensive device called a toilet dam can make a big difference. It blocks off part of the tank, so that it holds and uses less water—about two to two-and-a-half gallons less per flush. For a family of four, this can amount to well over 10,000 gallons less water used per year, tremendous savings for a device that costs between five and ten dollars.

There is great potential for water conservation in your yard. Plant drought-resistant varieties of plants and grass. Especially in the summer, keep your grass a little longer (set your lawn mower for a height of about three inches). You may need to mow a little more often, but longer grass needs less water and survives hot temperatures better. Also, aerate your yard. Holes from aeration help the water soak into the ground faster, so that more of it is used by your lawn and plants and less is lost to evaporation. Water your lawn before 10:00 A.M. Afternoon watering leads to more loss thorough evaporation and can promote mold growth. It may be worthwhile to invest in a timer for your hose so that you can set it to water for a specific length of time. There are some that work like an egg timer (without electricity) and are easy to install between your faucet and the hose. In general, it's better for grass to receive a really thorough watering (for two hours or so) once a week than more shallow watering on a more frequent basis. Watering deeply at longer intervals encourages stronger root growth, which makes the grass less vulnerable to heat and dehydration. Likewise, using mulch around flowers, shrubs, and vegetable gardens also conserves water—and can save you money.

When we try to figure out where all our money goes, the simple, everyday things like laundry and water use don't usually come to mind. But you'll be astonished how much money you can save if you combine all of the simple suggestions above: keep energy and water use to a minimum when doing laundry, reduce the setting of your water heater and keep it working efficiently, and use less water—especially hot water—in every way you can.

LIGHTING

About 15 percent of the electricity used in the home goes for lighting, and most Americans waste a good portion of this amount by overlighting and by leaving lights on when they are not needed. Therefore, the simplest steps you can take to reduce your lighting expenses are to turn off and cut back; that is, turn off lights when they're unnecessary and cut back on the wattage used. You will immediately save money on your electric bill, and since the bulbs will last longer, you will eventually save on the purchase of bulbs also.

Study the living patterns in your home and decide where bright lighting is required: for reading and working areas, and for areas where safety is a consideration, like stairwells, outside walks, etc. Then systematically check out each lighting fixture to determine its appropriateness. Do you really need that three-light fixture in a room where you watch television, for example?

Decide whether you should choose incandescent or fluorescent lighting. Incandescent bulbs use much more energy than fluorescent bulbs. They also radiate 75 percent of the energy they use in the form of heat (another reason to turn off unnecessary incandescent lighting). For that same reason, you probably don't want incandescent bulbs in your kitchen, since the stove, dishwasher, refrigerator, and other appliances all generate heat. Fluorescent lights are at least three times more efficient than incandescent bulbs, and can last ten times longer. Fluorescent lighting works particularly well over the kitchen sink and counters, in bath and dressing areas, and over a workbench or playing area. As you plan your lighting strategy, consider the following suggestions.

Turn off all lights when you leave a room, even if you're going to be gone for only a few minutes. Many people think that you should leave a fluorescent light on unless you're going to be out of the room for at least half an hour, because otherwise the starter will burn out.

However, thanks to advances in technology, these starters, which used to be expensive, are now quite inexpensive, making it more energy efficient to turn off *all* lights whenever you leave the room.

Consider buying compact fluorescent bulbs— which are relatively new and have built-in adapters that allow them to be used in ordinary nonfluorescent fixtures—to replace your incandescent bulbs. Compact fluorescents cost more than regular light bulbs, so you may not be able to afford to replace all your bulbs at once, but with each bulb you replace you will save enough money over time to more than make up for the price difference. According to one estimate, each 100-watt compact fluorescent you install will yield about twenty-five dollars in savings over the life of the bulb. Compact fluorescents are larger than standard light bulbs, and come in a variety of shapes, so make sure you get the appropriate one for your fixture. Also, you cannot use these bulbs in a fixture linked to a dimmer switch, where they pose a risk of fire, or with clip-on lampshades, which will puncture the bulb. If you can't find compact fluorescent bulbs with built-in adapters, check your local hardware store for separate adapters that will allow you to install ordinary fluorescent bulbs in your existing fixtures.

If you use the same room for a variety of activities, save energy by installing and using three-way light bulbs. The light level can then be set at its brightest for reading or sewing and at a lower setting for watching television, chatting, or just lounging.

Purchase low-energy, high-efficiency incandescent light bulbs, which offer more light for less energy. A watt is the unit for measuring the energy used, and a lumen is the measurement for the amount of light produced. The higher the lumens number, the more light produced. Newer, more efficient bulbs can give you the lumens of a 100-watt bulb for the energy needed to light a regular 75-watt bulb.

Avoid multisocket fixtures. If your house has a number of two- or three-socket fixtures in locations where low light levels are adequate, remove one of the bulbs and replace it with a burned-out bulb for safety (or simply don't replace a bulb the next time one burns out). In locations where bright lighting is required, use a single higher wattage bulb rather than two or more bulbs of lower wattage (instead of two 60-watt bulbs in an overhead light, switch to only one 100-watt bulb).

Keep all lamps, bulbs, and fixtures clean. As much as possible, when decorating, select light colors for ceilings, walls, curtains and drapes, carpet, and furniture. Lampshades that are lined in white and ceilings that are painted in lighter colors are particularly important in reflecting light and making a room brighter. Darker colors will absorb light and require more light and more energy.

Make sure the bottom edge of your lampshade is above your eye level if you are using a lamp for reading. If the lampshade is lower, it's doing a terrific job of lighting the table, but it's not helping your eyes.

Consider installing solid-state dimmer switches, which make it easy and convenient to alter the light level in a room.
Caution: Do not install dimmer switches in or linked to fixtures you've converted to fluorescent bulbs.

Turn off decorative outdoor gas or electric lamps unless they are needed for safety. Eight gaslights burning for one year use enough gas to heat a typical home for a winter; depending on where you live, each lamp may cost as much as four dollars per month to operate.

If outdoor lighting is a necessity, install a timer or photocell unit that will turn the lights on and off automatically.

As with other aspects of controlling your expenditures, managing energy costs in your home demands careful planning and considered action. It is not sufficient to allow "things" to take their usual course because the result will inevitably be wasted energy—and more expensive bills for you. However, if you're willing to apply some of the suggestions I've made here and, just as important, use my suggestions as an inspiration to learn and improve your own energy quotient, or EQ, then you *can* create significant savings—of your money, which can then be put to better use, and of our precious natural resources. I guarantee you'll feel warmer all over.

7

Cutting Car Costs

For years, most Americans have enjoyed the luxury of driving almost everywhere they go; books and movies have been written about this "love affair" with the automobile, which apparently is a uniquely American phenomenon. Learning to drive a car is a skill that most teenagers start to acquire soon after their fifteenth birthday, and obtaining a driver's license has long been established as one of the few important initiation rituals still surviving in our complex, urbanized society. Many people consider their automobile an extension of their personality, and clearly a great deal of prestige can be associated with the type of car you drive.

Yet driving an automobile has become increasingly expensive, not just because of the cost of automobiles themselves, but also because of the cost of the insurance, the inevitable repairs and maintenance, and the increasing cost of fuel. Next to your home, your car probably will be the single most expensive item you and your family will own. Do not allow yourself to be seduced by the American "love affair"—at least not until you possess a substantial amount of discretionary income. Until then, you must view a car as expensive transportation, and nothing else. And as with any other major expense, you should carefully examine all of your options.

First and foremost, you should consider reducing your reliance on a car by carpooling and using public transportation. If the occupancy in cars commuting to work were to increase by just one person per car, more than 40 million gallons of gas—or more than $40 million— would be saved *each day*. As our roads become more clogged and our air gets more polluted, many employers and communities are trying to make these options more attractive to people. For example, many communities now offer park-and-ride lots that allow commuters to meet at a public parking lot, leave their cars, and carpool or take mass transit. Some companies reserve special parking spaces closer to the building for carpoolers. And some employers create special work arrangements for employees who use mass transit, such as earlier starting and quitting times, to accommodate their transportation schedules. Some even offer financial incentives. Most mass transit systems offer a cheaper monthly, weekly, or multiple-use rate for commuters and others who use them frequently. In addition, many systems offer discounts for students or senior citizens. Find out what options may be available to you.

In addition to carpooling and using public transportation, there are two other alternatives you should consider— walking and bicycling—that don't involve gasoline, nor do they pollute the air. Besides saving money on fuel, you get exercise that could lead to savings on your health costs.

If you're like most Americans, though, driving a car is not just a luxury, it's a necessity. If you need to purchase a car and you are serious about trying to pinch your pennies, then you must learn as much as possible about buying, insuring, and maintaining a car, and then take creative measures to minimize how much you spend.

BUYING A CAR

When you begin thinking about buying a car: Stop! look! and listen! Remember that old warning from your mother about crossing the street? Well, cars can be dangerous in more ways than one. If you're not careful, cars can run you over financially as well as physically.

First of all, make certain you really *need* to buy a car and are not just being lured by the gleaming metal and the prestige of driving a fancy machine that talks to you when you open the door. (It's okay to buy a car as a toy, but only if you can afford a toy that costs that much.) Then write down a list of priorities to consider in selecting a car. Do you commute long distances to work and need a larger, safer, and more comfortable car? Will the car be driven mainly in short forays around town and therefore gulp gas, suggesting you should look closely at the fuel efficiency ratings? You should decide at this point—*before* you begin shopping—which options aren't really necessary for your specific needs and which ones you definitely need. Are you really so lonely that you need a car that talks back to you, or would you rather spend the money on comfortable seats? Do you really need that five-speaker sound system that can be heard three blocks away? Or would you rather spend that money on better tires? Is an automatic transmission absolutely necessary, or could you adapt to driving a stick shift? Would you suffocate without air conditioning where you live, or is that really a luxury you'd probably use for only one or two weeks out of the year? If safety is an important factor in your decision, then you should rate your car choices based on the availability of safety equipment, like air bags and antilock brakes, both of which have been proven to save lives.

Once you have determined what qualities are important in a car—what you *need*, not necessarily what you *want*—then you face another big decision: What can you afford to pay? Presumably by now you have a budget and have figured out where the money is going to come from, and you have reckoned how much you will have to sacrifice in order to buy your car. Hopefully you have saved a big chunk of the money, and if you already own a car, you can sell it to serve as part of the down payment. But be aware that the cost of a car is always more than the sticker price. Before making your decision, check with your insurance company to find out how expensive the cars you're interested in are to insure. If possible, talk with people you know who already own the models you've selected, and consult consumer magazines for their assessment of your selections' reliability. You also must decide at this point if you want a new or previously owned vehicle; you don't want to buy a used car that's going to spend most of its time in the shop, but remember, you pay heavily for the privilege of saying, "It's brand new."

You may want to check out leasing as an alternative, also, especially if you have a problem coming up with a down payment. With most leases there is little or no down payment required, and the monthly lease payments are usually less than what you would pay if purchasing. You should be aware, however, that leasing contracts usually limit the number of miles you can drive per year without a penalty (normally 15,000), and when the lease expires you will have nothing: no car, and no equity in the car to trade in on another vehicle. Leasing an auto is seldom to your advantage, except in a few special cases or unless you receive exceptional terms.

The next step is to position yourself to make the best possible deal on the car of your choice. Recently, General

Motors' Saturn dealers have been successful in promoting "no-haggle" buying. There has been some speculation that this will initiate a trend that will spread across the country, but as of this writing only about 2 percent of the dealerships in the United States have nonnegotiable sticker prices. With the other 98 percent, the only way to make certain you receive the best deal available in your area of the country is to do your homework, shop around, and be flexible. Keep in mind these points as you search for your next car.

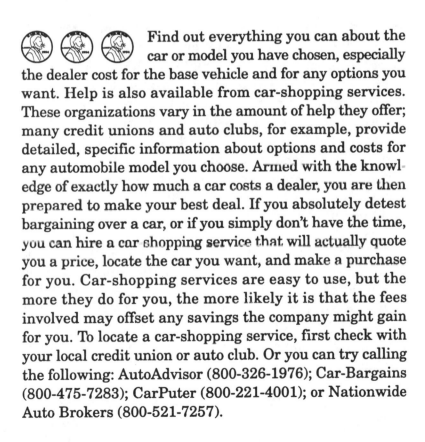 Find out everything you can about the car or model you have chosen, especially the dealer cost for the base vehicle and for any options you want. Help is also available from car-shopping services. These organizations vary in the amount of help they offer; many credit unions and auto clubs, for example, provide detailed, specific information about options and costs for any automobile model you choose. Armed with the knowledge of exactly how much a car costs a dealer, you are then prepared to make your best deal. If you absolutely detest bargaining over a car, or if you simply don't have the time, you can hire a car shopping service that will actually quote you a price, locate the car you want, and make a purchase for you. Car-shopping services are easy to use, but the more they do for you, the more likely it is that the fees involved may offset any savings the company might gain for you. To locate a car-shopping service, first check with your local credit union or auto club. Or you can try calling the following: AutoAdvisor (800-326-1976); Car-Bargains (800-475-7283); CarPuter (800-221-4001); or Nationwide Auto Brokers (800-521-7257).

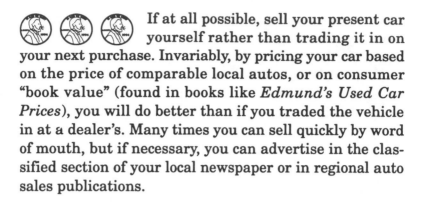 If at all possible, sell your present car yourself rather than trading it in on your next purchase. Invariably, by pricing your car based on the price of comparable local autos, or on consumer "book value" (found in books like *Edmund's Used Car Prices*), you will do better than if you traded the vehicle in at a dealer's. Many times you can sell quickly by word of mouth, but if necessary, you can advertise in the classified section of your local newspaper or in regional auto sales publications.

Be prepared *before* you approach dealers. In addition to knowing what model and options you want, you should know how much you are willing to pay. The sticker price is seldom of much value in arriving at a fair price. Study car-pricing guides, which are available at your newsstand, public library, or credit union, and which are published in magazines such as *Kiplinger's Personal Finance Magazine*, to determine the invoiced or dealer cost for the car you wish to purchase. You should then calculate your offer at approximately 3 or 4 percent above dealer cost.

Once you have determined a fair offer based on dealer cost, plan on sticking to your price. Visit as many dealers in your area as it takes until one is willing to do business on your terms. Shop at the end of the month, when dealers are more eager to close out inventory and salespeople are pushing to meet their quotas.

   When you have an offer(s) under consideration by a dealer, take your price to other dealers and ask them to match or beat it. It never hurts to let Dealer A know that you are about to close a deal with a Dealer B. Ask Dealer A straight out if they want your business, and if so, what they are willing to do to secure the sale.

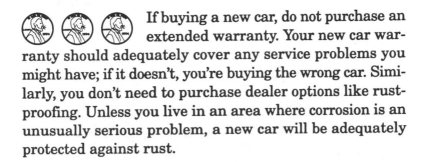 If buying a new car, do not purchase an extended warranty. Your new car warranty should adequately cover any service problems you might have; if it doesn't, you're buying the wrong car. Similarly, you don't need to purchase dealer options like rustproofing. Unless you live in an area where corrosion is an unusually serious problem, a new car will be adequately protected against rust.

Shop around for the best deal on financing *before* you conclude your negotiations to purchase a car. In most cases, your local bank or credit union will be glad to finance your loan for you, and they will usually tell you how much they will finance ahead of time. If you have an existing home equity loan, or can qualify for one, you should consider borrowing the money that way, since the interest on an auto loan is not tax-deductible, but interest on a home equity loan is. The finance officer at the auto dealership will encourage you to buy disability and life insurance—and add the premiums to your loan payments—but unless you don't have insurance, this is an unnecessary expense.

INSURING YOUR CAR

Insurance is the next major expense after purchasing your car. Having automobile insurance is compulsory in most states. If you're uninsured or underinsured, and have an accident, it may cost more than you possess to pay medical bills, car repairs, legal fees, and court costs. Since most of us have no choice but to have auto insurance, and since its cost continues to increase quite rapidly, we must try to pinch pennies in order to survive.

The price of your automobile insurance depends on a number of factors. In determining your premiums, insurance companies consider a driver's age, sex, marital status, length of time as a driver, driving record, the age and model of the car, the amount of coverage necessary, and the amount of the deductible. Because the statistics of risk govern the decisions made by insurance companies, certain types of drivers are considered a higher risk and must pay a higher premium. One high-risk group is unmarried men under twenty-five (although women in that age group are rapidly closing the gender gap). Another high-risk group consists of drivers who have been driving less than three years, even if they've had no accidents.

A poor driving record will, of course, raise the cost of your insurance. The more accidents and moving traffic violations you have had, the higher your insurance premiums. The type of automobile you're insuring is also a factor. A more expensive car costs more to insure because the insurance company would have to pay out more to replace it. Cars with high-performance engines, a "racing" or sports car look, and some trucks require higher premiums also, because statistics show they are more likely to be involved in accidents. Some cars are more likely to be targets for theft. It's not easy to determine the insurance rating of a particular model, so you must rely on your insurance agent. Once you have narrowed down your model choices, phone your agent and request the ratings and costs *before* you proceed to the dickering stage with the car dealer.

A typical automobile insurance policy is complex and filled with clauses and heretofores. Many people fail to submit claims because they don't really understand what the policy covers and doesn't cover. Types of insurance vary from state to state, but basically, most auto insurance coverage falls into four categories. Depending on the state you live in, either *liability* or *no-fault* insurance is available, and most likely required. In some states, liability coverage pays for other people's bodily injuries and damage to property (including vehicles) if you are found liable for an accident. In other states, no-fault coverage allows you to collect payment for damage or injury from your insurance company regardless of who is at fault. *Collision* coverage pays for damage to your vehicle caused by a moving accident if it is the only car involved. *Comprehensive* coverage pays for damage to your vehicle caused by something other than a moving accident (fire, theft, flying objects, flood, etc.). Each type of coverage allows certain minimums, and you pay higher premiums as your amount of coverage increases. Examine your policy carefully, and then ask your agent about those points of coverage you don't understand. Remember, the only stupid question is the one you don't ask, and you may be paying extra for coverage you don't really need. Here are some other ways you can lower your auto insurance premiums.

Drive defensively and wear your seat belt. With the frequency and cost of accidents as high as they are today, driving defensively is much more than a nice slogan. Pay attention to conditions and people around you, try to anticipate other drivers' moves, and avoid accidents even if it means being late occasionally or suffering indignities from other drivers. A good driving record over a five-year period may earn you a discount on your insurance, and you may save your own or someone else's life in the process. Some insurance companies will give you a discount for a good driving record plus another discount if you have your home insured with their company as well.

Increase the deductible on your collision coverage. A deductible of $250 means you'll pay the first $250 of a repair bill, and the insurance company will pay the remainder. If you have a small accident that costs less for repairs than your deductible, you have to cover all the expenses out of pocket, and the cost to your insurance company is zero. You might save as much as 30 percent on your premium if you increase the deductible from $100 to $500. Since I believe insurance should be used to prevent financial ruin by covering large expenses, and not be used for petty "fender benders," I recommend you increase your deductible to $500 if your financial situation allows it. If you own an older car that has been depreciated to under $1,000, you should consider dropping collision insurance entirely.

On the other hand, I recommend that you increase your liability limits (in those states with liability coverage) to *at least* $250,000 for bodily injury and $50,000 for property damage. If you suffer an accident that causes injury, the medical and legal costs can be catastrophic. The extra premium you pay for this insurance will reward you with the peace of mind that, should you ever be in a serious accident, you will have some chance of surviving financially.

MAINTAINING AND DRIVING YOUR CAR

How well you take care of your automobile can determine how long you have it and how much it costs you to operate over the years. Basic maintenance such as tune-ups and oil changes will keep your car running efficiently, save fuel, and save you money on more costly repairs. You may even want to learn how to do some of these basic jobs yourself by taking a course at your local adult education program. If you do take your car to a mechanic, try to take it to the same one each time. Cultivate a relationship with your mechanic so that he or she knows you as a regular customer, and so you can trust the mechanic to treat you fairly. A mechanic who sees your car regularly can keep accurate records, and a reputable garage will guarantee any work done. In addition, if you're a regular customer, a mechanic can give you plenty of notice if you should need any major repair work done; then you can plan for it and perhaps save money. The following tips can save you hundreds, perhaps thousands, of dollars a year.

Read your owner's manual, especially the section on regularly scheduled maintenance. Then follow the schedule. Changing the oil, tuning the engine, and many other routine chores should be performed at the recommended intervals. Don't assume that if your car seems to be running fine, you can skip the maintenance. On the other hand, don't assume that you must take your car to the dealership's shop for routine maintenance, even if your car is covered by a manufacturer's warranty. You can perform many of the routine maintenance tasks yourself, such as changing the oil, inspecting belts, flushing the radiator, and changing air filters, or you can have these done by any service garage you choose. As long as you document the date and mileage on the odometer when the service is performed, your warranty should remain in effect.

If you purchase a new car, follow the manufacturer's suggestions regarding a break-in period. Many manuals instruct buyers to alter the way they drive—not to exceed certain speeds, to vary driving speed, etc.—for the first 1,000 miles or so. Failure to heed the break-in instructions can damage the car and lead to complete engine breakdown.

Think about how you drive. Do you stomp on the gas pedal, then stomp on the brake? Does your car purr, or does it roar when you drive? The way you drive can greatly affect your gas mileage. If you stomp on your gas pedal, you're burning extra gas unnecessarily. Use gentle, steady pressure on the gas and brake pedals to save gas, to decrease wear on your engine, and to extend the life of your brakes and tires. Anticipate stops and begin stopping *before* you reach the stoplight or the traffic jam. If you have cruise control, use it on the highway to maintain a steady speed at the posted speed limit. The average car uses about 17 percent less gasoline at 55 miles per hour than it does at 65. (You should use your cruise control only when you're alert enough to maintain complete concentration on the road. If you fall asleep in cruise control, the only thing that will stop your car will be the obstacle it collides with.) For city driving, a speed between 30 and 40 miles per hour is advised. Driving closer to 30 will save gas. You may *save* a minute or two by driving faster— but you *spend* more money.

Plan your excursions for the most efficient use of gas, and take care of as many chores as possible at the same time. If you have a lot of errands to do, write down where you want to go and picture your route as a big loop. Try to plan when you'll go to each place according to where it's located in the loop. The most efficient plan is one in which the last errand is the one closest to your house on the way home.

Call first before going out. You can save yourself a trip if you find out that the order isn't ready, the store's closed, or the flight's been delayed. Also, when shopping for a major purchase, it really does pay to "let your fingers do the shopping." It can save you hours in stores—and money in gas.

Avoid stop-and-go driving. The longer you sit in traffic, the more gas you use. Try to find an alternate route or time your travel so you can avoid the heavier traffic.

Don't sit still with your engine running. Most cars today don't need to "warm up" unless you have extremely cold temperatures (about the amount of time it takes to fasten your seat belt is usually sufficient). If you're going to be idling for more than two or three minutes, turn off the engine. It uses less gas to restart the engine than it does to keep it running. If you drive up to a teller's window or a fast-food window, turn off your engine out of courtesy as well as to save gas.

 Carry a telephone book and a map in your car. If you get lost, you can check your map or call for directions. If you're planning a trip, look for maps of the areas you will be driving through before you leave. Many auto clubs provide a routing service in which they will plan your entire trip for you, suggesting the best highways, motels, and restaurants, and giving you money-saving tips as well.

Keep your tires properly inflated to keep them in good condition longer. An overinflated tire increases the risk of a puncture and consequently an accident. An underinflated tire will make your car drag and increase your gas usage by as much as 0.4 percent for each pound of pressure it is underinflated.

Uneven tire wear can indicate a need for new shock absorbers. It can also be a reminder of a previous puncture, however. Before you decide to go ahead and get new shocks, think about whether you've had that tire repaired. You may be spending money needlessly.

Learn some basic repair measures that can save you towing charges. You should learn where the fuse compartment is located, and make certain you have spare fuses. Find the jack that's hidden away in the trunk and figure out how to use it. You might even want to practice changing a tire in advance, so that if you ever need to do it in an emergency, you'll be prepared. Always carry a flashlight or lantern and flares so that you can see and be seen at night, or to signal for help. If you know how to change the belts in your car, carry an emergency replacement in your trunk. Stow a roll of high-quality rubber electrical tape in the trunk; you'll be surprised at how many uses you may have for it. For example, if a

hose ruptures, many times you can tape the leak secure-
ly enough to get to the next service station. Without the
temporary seal, you would have to pay for a tow. I learned
another technique for temporarily repairing a leak in the
gas tank. A friend of mine suggested carrying a bar of soap
in the car. You rub the soap over the puncture; the soap
melts, forming a temporary patch, and you can get to the
garage for repairs. (In order for this to work, you have to
use plain, ordinary soap that has no scents or other cosmetic additives.)

Carry jumper cables in your car and know how
to use them in case of an emergency. Move the
car with the live battery close enough so that the cables
reach, but not so close that the two cars are touching.
Clamp the end of one cable (usually red) to the positive
terminal (+ side) of the weak battery, and attach the other
end to the positive terminal of the strong battery. Attach
one clamp from the other cable (usually black) to the negative terminal of the strong battery, then attach the other
end to an unpainted bolt on the engine of the weak car—
not to the weak battery, or you may have an explosion.
Check to make sure the cables won't get caught in any
mechanism when the cars are started. When both cars are
running, remove the cables in the reverse order from which
you attached them. Run the weak car for awhile to re-
charge the battery.

Save money by pumping your gas yourself and paying in cash. Most service stations charge less if you
pump the gas, check the oil, and clean the windshield yourself. Many stations also offer lower prices if you pay in
cash instead of by credit card.

Know what type of gas works best for your car. Octane is a measure of how resistant a fuel is to premature ignition, or "spark knocking." It is not a measure of the power in the gasoline. Some cars need a higher octane gas to run more efficiently, but if so the owner's manual should state the required octane. Although some advertisements try to make you believe otherwise, there is usually no advantage to burning high-octane gas (except as stated in the manual). Sometimes the gas required depends on your tune-up, so you might have to ask your mechanic about it. The alcohol content of the gas you use can also affect your car's performance. We once bought a less expensive unleaded fuel and our gas mileage went down. Our car wasn't tuned for the higher alcohol content of that fuel.

Remember that the extra gadgets in your car contribute to a decrease in gas mileage. Extras like your cigarette lighter, fan, air conditioner, defroster, heater, and radio can eat up fuel. It's impossible to avoid using them completely, but minimizing their use can add up to dollars in savings.

If you live in an extremely cold climate, consider buying an engine-block heater, a device that plugs into an electrical outlet to warm up your car's engine before you start it. The most stressful time for an engine is when it is first started, especially in cold weather, because the oil doesn't begin to circulate properly until it warms up. Using an engine-block heater allows the oil to warm up before you start the car, thus lubricating moving parts, reducing engine wear, and extending the life of your car. It can also cut your car's carbon monoxide emissions during warmup by as much as 80 percent!

Most of today's cars are expensive to buy, expensive to insure, and expensive to operate. In addition, like almost everything else in our modern world, automobiles have become so complicated that it is difficult if not impossible for the nonspecialist to understand how they work—much less attempt to repair them. And, unfortunately, the auto repair industry is not always trustworthy. In fact, according to the Council of Better Business Bureaus, auto mechanics consistently rank among the top six businesses that draw complaints from disgruntled customers. For you, the average consumer, this means that your best option is to avoid repair shops as much as possible. Buy smart, drive smart, and maintain your vehicle at peak efficiency. If major repairs do become necessary, always get a second opinion. Always try to speak to your mechanic personally. A mechanic has a much better chance of fixing your car if you can explain the problem directly; more importantly, if you can develop a trusting relationship with the mechanic, chances are that both you and your vehicle will be better cared for. In the long term, because purchasing and maintaining a vehicle is such an expensive process, you will discover numerous opportunities to pinch pennies—and save dollars.

8

Communication on a Budget

Most people spend a great deal of money each year to communicate with friends and family. There are a variety of ways to get your message to its destination, such as telephoning, writing letters, and sending packages. I certainly wouldn't suggest that you save money by *not* communicating with friends and relatives, but there are ways that you can keep in touch for less with just a minimum of effort on your part.

THE TELEPHONE

The ubiquitous telephone is arguably the most important communication tool since smoke signals. Trying to imagine a world without the telephone, and without the other means of communication that rely on telephone lines, is virtually impossible in our society. Most of us take the telephone so much for granted that we hardly pause to consider if we could do without it, and we pay our phone bills as routinely as we do our food or fuel bills. Yet there is hardly anything that is conveyed by telephone that could not be communicated using other, more economical means. This is especially true if you subscribe to all the frills that now seem to be inevitably "hooked" to the phone: expensive designer phones, car phones, remote phones, fax machines, answering machines, call waiting, call forwarding, call screening—the directory of phone apparatus and services goes on and on. Do you really need all this fancy—and expensive—equipment and services? What are your options, and have you explored ways that you can save money on your phone bills? As you examine your individual communication needs, keep the following points in mind.

Purchase your telephones rather than renting them from the telephone company. The initial purchase of the equipment may cost some money, but you'll spend much less in the long run, since renting means you pay an amount every month for years. It's also possible to buy your equipment less expensively and save even more. Look for sales and for equipment that has been reconditioned.

If you have a problem with your phone, check it out yourself before you call for repair. If a telephone company technician comes and finds out that the problem is with your equipment, you will be charged for the house call (at least fifty dollars). If you have more than one phone in your home, or a computer, answering machine, or fax machine hooked up to a phone line, one of these items may be interfering with the rest of your phones. Start by unplugging all the appliances that are hooked to your phone line (except for one telephone). Then have a friend call you. If that phone doesn't work, unplug it and try another phone. If the second one works, the problem is the first phone. If you have only one phone, see if you can borrow one from a friend to help you determine whether your phone is broken or not. If none of the phones you try works and you can't find a loose wire or connection (since the current carried by phone lines is not dangerous, you can check any accessible wiring inside the house), the problem is most likely your incoming phone lines. Most phone companies will repair problems on the lines outside of your house for free, but will charge you for repairs on phone wiring inside your house. Your phone company probably offers a maintenance plan for inside wiring for a nominal monthly fee.

Thoroughly study the packages offered by local and long-distance phone companies to determine the most economical system for your needs. Since the breakup of AT&T, you have the option of shopping around for the best rates for your long-distance service. Some companies offer a discount after you've made a certain number of calls. Others charge a flat monthly fee, and that amount is added to your bill regardless of how many calls you make. Some companies give a bigger discount when you make calls to other people who also subscribe to that company. In most places, you must designate which long-distance phone company you want to deal with, but you can always change companies if your needs change. (Keep in mind, however, that there may be a charge on your local phone bill for switching over.)

Learn when the lowest rates for long-distance calling are in effect, and practice smart calling. In most places, long-distance calls are cheaper if you call between 5:00 and 11:00 P.M. The cheapest rates are usually between 11:00 P.M. and 5:00 A.M. and on weekends and holidays.

Eliminate equipment and services that you don't use. Your local phone bill usually includes a basic charge plus charges for any extra services you have. Extras can include touch-tone service, a personalized number, call waiting, call forwarding, three-way calling, call blocking, etc. Some people really need some of these extras, but most people try a novelty service and then forget about it. If you find options you don't need on your statement, call the phone company and cancel them. Why pay for something you don't need?

Avoid using directory assistance. Instead, look up numbers for yourself in the telephone directory. If you frequently call numbers in an area not included in your directory, contact the telephone company to request the directory for that area. Additional directories are often available free if you request them. If you must call for local directory assistance, be aware that it is sometimes possible to do so free of charge if you call from a public telephone, even though you would have to pay for this service if you called from home.

If you have children or teenagers, consider a service that "locks out" 900 or 976 numbers from your phones. With the current blitz of television ads for pay-for-phone services, children and teenagers (and many adults) may be tempted to call these numbers, not realizing how much the bills will be—and they can be substantial. This can be worthwhile even if you don't have children who abuse these numbers. We once found ourselves stuck with a fee for three calls we never made simply because the phone company couldn't get back the money they paid to the electronic bulletin board whose number was on our phone bill. We had not made these calls, and our children were then too small to use the phone. Obviously, someone else had charged the calls to our number. We got a "lock" put on our phone line, and since then there have been no surprise numbers on our bill.

If unwarranted charges appear on your telephone bill, phone the telephone company as soon as possible and explain the situation. You may not have to pay for calls for which you are not responsible.

If you're calling from a hotel or motel, or to the United States from another country, find out whether it's cheaper to call collect or direct, or to use a phone other than the one in your room. Many hotels add a surcharge for long-distance calls made from your room, regardless of whether you make a direct, collect, or credit card call. This surcharge can amount to a substantial sum, so you should instead find the nearest pay phone and select your own long-distance company. Sometimes the local currency-to-dollar ratio makes it cheaper to make a collect call. When my husband and I were stationed in Japan, it cost twice as much to call direct to the United States from Japan as it did the other way around; I had an agreement with my parents that if I called collect, they would keep track of the charges and I would reimburse them later.

POSTAL SERVICE

A less expensive way to communicate with friends and relatives is through the mail. In addition to the standard letter or card, there are many imaginative ways to get your message through by mail—you can send audiotapes, videotapes, and packages. I have found that on many occasions these other methods seem more meaningful than tele-phoning, probably because they give the recipient some-thing tangible to hold onto and treasure. Investigate the costs and rewards of keeping in touch by sending letters and other surprises through the mail, at least some of the time, perhaps beginning with a letter to a special friend or relative. As you start your alternative communication program, remember the following hints.

Use the exact postage. Currently, the postage for a one-ounce letter is twenty-nine cents. If the letter is over one-quarter inch thick, you must add another ten cents for an oversized package. If your letter weighs over one ounce, add twenty-three cents more for each added ounce. Some people just add another 29-cent stamp for the second ounce, which means they pay an extra six cents in postage unnecessarily. Although wasting six cents might not seem like much, I hope by now you have realized how those pennies, if saved with your other pennies, add up quickly to dollars and much more.

If you're sending a letter overseas, use the most eco-nomical means. It currently costs fifty cents per half-ounce to send a letter out of the United States. Air-mail paper will help keep the weight down. An even less expen-sive way to send a letter overseas is to use an aerogram, which is a piece of paper that folds into an envelope and has the postage imprinted on it.

Forward mail without paying additional postage. If you or someone close to you moves around a great deal, there is always a problem with forwarding the mail. When my husband was in the military, my mother-in-law used to put his mail into another envelope and pay more postage to send it to him. Of course, this wasn't necessary. All she needed to do was cross out her address and write "Please forward," along with his new address, on the letters and put them back in the mail. (The envelope must not be opened before this is done. Mail that has been opened and resealed requires new postage.) When you change addresses, fill out a change-of-address card at the post office, and the postal service will forward your mail automatically for one year at no charge.

If you receive merchandise in the mail that you don't want, and you know it before you open the package, cross out your address and write, "Return to sender—merchandise refused" on the box and put it back in the mail. (Don't break the seal or open the invoice; if you do, you will need new postage.) This way you not only save the payment you would have made for the unwanted merchandise, you also save the return postage.

Buy and mail an hour-long audiocassette, putting your letter—and anyone else's letter—on it; the cost can be less than that for a phone call. There are special cassette mailers on the market for your convenience. A tape weighs about two ounces, so postage is sixty-two cents: twenty-nine cents for the first ounce, twenty-three cents for the second ounce, and ten cents for being over one-quarter inch thick. Your friend or relative can then use the same cassette to send you a return letter.

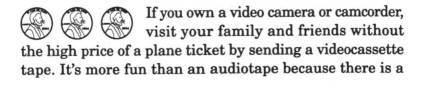

If you own a video camera or camcorder, visit your family and friends without the high price of a plane ticket by sending a videocassette tape. It's more fun than an audiotape because there is a picture with your letter. Sending a videocassette tape may cost as much as a phone call, but you can get two to six hours on a tape, and it, too, can be reused. Seal the tape in a sturdy box to avoid damage. Make sure you put a notation on the box that says, "Do not x-ray—contains videotape," to avoid the possibility that your tape will be erased.

For a real treat, mail your friend or family member a package. The United States Postal Service has different rates for different services. First class is the fastest (about four days for delivery), but it's also the most expensive. A first-class package may weigh up to seventy pounds and be up to 108 inches in length and girth combined. Second class is used by businesses and magazines. Third class may weigh up to one pound. Parcel Post or fourth class has the same size limitations as first class, but it's slower (six to ten days for delivery). Book rate may be less expensive than other rates, but as the name implies, it's limited to books and records. Check out all your options and compare the prices. Depending on the package and other factors, sometimes there's only a five- or ten-cent difference in price between first class and fourth class; at other times the difference is a matter of dollars.

When you're mailing a package overseas, decide whether you want to send it surface delivery or by air. Surface mail is less expensive, but it may take months instead of weeks for your package to arrive. Before you send out your package, check the International Mailing Manual at the post office for the country to which you're mailing. If you try to send certain things that are considered to be contraband into some countries—even though the items are perfectly legal in the United States—their customs officials may confiscate the whole package and not just the forbidden material. Fill out a customs slip, and depending on the contents, pay for insurance on your package. A lost package is easier and less expensive to track down if it's insured.

Make sure your package is properly packed for mailing. If it rattles at the beginning of its journey and is broken at the end, you may not get reimbursed for it because it was improperly packed. Also, always make sure to put the name and address of the recipient on the inside as well as the outside of your package. If you don't, and if the label becomes unreadable, your package may end up at the dead letter office.

If you insure a package, keep track of your receipts. In case the package is lost, you will need to prove how much the contents of the package were worth by showing sales slips. You will also need to keep track of your insurance receipt until the package gets to its destination, because the receipt has the number that identifies the package and the date you sent it.

Here is a note for people who use the mailbox as a drop box for nonmail items. Legally, "your" mailbox is the property of the U.S. Postal Service. If anything other than mail is deposited in it, you are breaking the law. Anyone who puts a nonmail item in a mailbox is liable for a fine, which can be as little as the postage that would be required to send the item through the mail, or as much as $500. If you need a drop box, put up a second box and clearly label it "Not for mail."

Unlike many of the other areas I have discussed, the amount of money you spend on communicating with your friends and relatives is solely a matter of personal choice. This amount depends to a large extent on the way you feel about maintaining open lines of communication. You might, for example, feel that phoning or writing long-distance friends is a waste of money, especially if your budget is very tight. In that case, you might be tempted to ignore the penny-pinching tips here, feeling that you will avoid all or most of these expenses simply by not keeping in close contact with friends and relatives.

In my opinion, that would be a mistake. Aside from the personal gratification and good feelings that can come from maintaining close relationships, there can be an added, *economic* gain from making those calls or sending those packages. As I pointed out earlier, the chief way you have of learning about bargains and new ways to save money is through a networking system—which is nothing more than people with common goals helping each other by communicating with each other. Similarly, if you are ever out of work, chances are that any leads you get that secure you a new job will be communicated to you by your friends and relatives. So using that telephone or the postal service to keep in touch might just be the best investment you can make. Think about it.

9
Enjoying Leisure Time For Less

Perhaps by now I've convinced you that if you work hard, budget your income, and spend smart, you can save enough to get ahead. But "all work and no play" is no fun. After all, why are you pinching pennies if you can't enjoy some of the benefits of your financial strategies once in a while? Certainly an important part of every budget is the amount set aside for travel and entertainment. I highly recommend that you take the time to enjoy yourself—and your family and friends—as often as possible, for then when you return to your normal routine you can be refreshed and better prepared to go back to work. What is important in savoring your leisure time, however—as with all of your other time—is that you utilize the same principles I have discussed before. *Educate* yourself to the nearly endless possibilities available to you for leisure activities, many of which can cost very little; *plan* your vacation or leisure activity so as to get the most for your money; and *budget* so that you know how much you can spend and where the time and money will come from. When you have less disposable income, it is especially important to follow this strategy. No matter how tight your budget, however, you don't have to abandon all thoughts of a family vacation, dining out, or ever seeing a movie, concert, or play again. There are ways to enjoy leisure time economically.

TRAVEL

Whether it's a brief weekend visit to a friend's home or that long-awaited excursion for a week or more, travel can be relaxing, educational, and invigorating. Travel can also be very expensive, and sometimes, if everything doesn't go well, you can return home feeling more worn out than when you left. Before you leave home, do some research so you'll be able to find the best places and prices, and so there will be as few "surprises" as possible on your trip. Even with the best planning, your travel is likely to cost more than you anticipated, and that's if all goes according to plan!

One way to begin is by writing to the relevant Chamber of Commerce and requesting information about the place you plan to visit. Most states have tourist information departments that will eagerly send you free maps, brochures, and other inviting tidbits. If your destination is overseas, you might request information through the consulate of the country you're planning to visit. If possible, talk to other people who have visited your intended vacation spot, asking especially about problems they encountered along the way. Investing in a tour book may guide you to the best bargains also. You don't have to plan your trip to the point of stifling all spontaneity, and you may not be able always to stick exactly to your budget. In general, though, you should have a plan and a budget— plus a built-in margin of variability. As you consider the following suggestions, remember that half the fun of any trip is in the planning and anticipation.

  Consider using a travel agency to help you with your plans. If you inform an agency ahead of time that you are planning a trip, agents can be on the alert for the best rates. Travel agents may be able to find a package deal or tour that will save you money, and an agent can prepare you for what to expect in accommodations, transportation, food, etc. Many times agencies can save you even more—50 percent or more—on special tours if you are willing to leave with little advance notice.

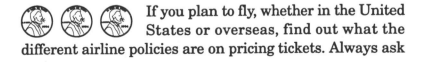 Decide ahead of time how you plan to pay your bills. This decision involves not only the important question of where the funds are coming from, but also the more practical issue of transferring money. If you're traveling more than fifty miles from home, your personal checks may not be accepted. You should not carry large sums of cash; if your money is lost, or if you are robbed (an increasingly likely prospect, unfortunately), you will simply suffer the loss—which will ruin your vacation and could play havoc with your other financial concerns, too. Alternatives are traveler's checks from a reputable company, credit cards, and automatic teller machines that are linked to your bank. Many banks, credit unions, and travel clubs now offer traveler's checks at little or no extra cost. I recommend that you carry travelor's checks for the bulk of your easy-access money, and rely on one good credit card (leave the others at home for security) as a backup and to charge large expenses like motel bills, auto rental, etc. That way, you can defer the payments for thirty days or more, with no interest charges (see Chapter 2, Managing Your Money).

If you plan to fly, whether in the United States or overseas, find out what the different airline policies are on pricing tickets. Always ask if any special fares are available, and under what conditions. If you buy well in advance (usually thirty days), fly midweek, fly at night, and/or stay for at least a specified period of time, you might be able to get a lower priced ticket. Be aware, though, that while some airlines will allow you to exchange a discounted ticket in an emergency for a nominal fee, most won't allow a refund for a discount fare under any circumstances.

Pack your bags with minimal necessities but don't stuff them. You certainly don't want to spend the money allocated for your vacation on shoes and underwear because you left them behind. On the other hand, you may want to bring back souvenirs without paying for excess weight. Make sure all your breakables and valuables are packed in your carry-on luggage to reduce the chance of breakage or loss.

If you check your baggage, make sure you remove any old destination tags, and put your name and where you can be reached inside your bags. These precautions can help you get your luggage back faster should you become separated.

If your chosen destination is within range, drive your car. Especially if you are traveling with family or friends, "getting there" becomes part of the fun. Of course, the time spent on the road becomes part of the vacation since you must pay for food and lodging. Investigate inexpensive motel chains that offer you basic accommodations at a reasonable price; some may give you an even better rate if you plan to stay at that chain's motels throughout your trip. Depending on your preferences, you might choose to save even more by camping out several nights and stopping at an inexpensive motel only occasionally. You can save on food by carrying plenty of nonperishables and a small cooler for perishables purchased along the way. Alternately, if you have only a night or so to relax, you might decide to spend most of your allocated funds on a fancy hotel, and make the hotel itself the attraction.

Look into bus and train travel as alternatives and ask about special fares or package deals. Here again, don't forget to budget for lodging if you are planning breaks in your ride. You might want to carry some nonperishables that you can supplement with a beverage when you stop for meals. If you're not in a hurry to get to your destination, you might enjoy the passing scenery and leave the driving to the operator of the bus or train.

Whether you fly or take a bus or train, you will probably need transportation when you arrive at your destination, which usually means renting a car. Find out if the airline, railroad, or bus line you're using offers any special deals with car rental agencies. If you have a friend where you are going, have him or her check around for the best price on a car rental. Compare the offered deals to determine which works best for your plans. Some rental agencies charge a set fee per day plus a specified amount for miles driven. Others offer a certain number of free miles per day, but if you drive more than that limit, you will be charged at a higher rate per mile. If you get a car with limited free mileage, budget your driving. As long as you stay within the miles per day multiplied by the number of days you rent the car, you can drive as many miles as you need on any one day.

Before you leave on your trip, find out if your regular car insurance policy covers your driving a rental car. If it does, you can save by not having to buy insurance through the rental agency. If you charge the rental fee to a major credit card, you may have insurance coverage included automatically.

If you are planning a trip to a foreign country, consider obtaining some of the foreign currency before you leave the United States (check with your local bank). Once you enter the foreign nation, you might not be able to cash a traveler's check right away, and it is always convenient to have enough local currency on hand for emergencies or for travel to your hotel. Also, exchange rates are usually least favorable at the airport, so having a little cash on hand will allow you to wait until you can shop around for the best exchange rate at the larger foreign banks before you convert many of your dollars. Rates are clearly posted.

When packing for a trip, make sure you pack an adequate supply of any medicines you use on a regular basis. This is especially important if you are traveling outside of the country, where obtaining the medicine you need may be difficult or impossible to do. Also, make sure your medicines are properly labeled. Don't mix medicines—especially prescription medicines—together in an unmarked bottle. If drugs are not labeled properly, they may be confiscated by customs. Worse, if you can't prove that you obtained certain medications legally, you could even end up in jail.

 If you are traveling to a foreign country, learn as much as you can about the local customs and laws. The federal government has a pamphlet called "Know Before You Go," available on request for international travelers. Talk to your travel agent and to anyone else who has been to the country you're planning to visit. Your ignorance could cost you a great deal of time and money, and could be dangerous as well.

If you are planning on traveling to a foreign country, make sure you have all the required shots *before* you leave the United States. You won't need them to get into the other country, but you will need them to get back into the U.S.

Although this type of travel doesn't have much to do with enjoyment, if there is a death in the family and you must travel to go to the funeral, ask your airline about bereavement fares. This is a tip I hope most readers won't need to use, but if you do, it can save you a substantial amount of money. Usually you must produce a copy of the death certificate (ask to have it wired or faxed to you) and proof of your relationship to the deceased to qualify for the lower fare.

DINING OUT

All of us like to eat out once in a while, but it is becoming a major expense to go to a nice restaurant or even to a family place. Undoubtedly you are familiar with the value available at restaurants in your own home town, and you can decide where to eat based on the occasion, who is along, how much you have to spend, and other factors. When you're dining in unfamiliar territory, however, whether in a neighboring city or in a foreign country, you must use all your resourcefulness to select a good value for your dollar. Just remember, anywhere you go there are restaurants that serve good food at reasonable prices; these are where the "locals" eat. Your task is to decide how much you want to pay and then find the appropriate restaurant. The following "tips" are for you—not for the server in the restaurant.

First, decide what kind of food you want and what price range you can afford. Many times you can solicit suggestions *before* you leave home. Family, friends, or coworkers are usually eager to pass on helpful information about enjoyable dining experiences they may have had in the location to which you're going. If you find yourself unprepared in an unfamiliar area, explain what kind of place you're looking for and ask your taxi driver, a bartender, a hotel concierge or doorman, or some other local resident what restaurants they would recommend.

Look for specials. Check newspapers, tourist guides, hotel directories, and other available sources to see if any restaurants have special offers like "early-bird specials," which give you a discount for eating between 4:00 and 6:00 P.M., when restaurants have fewer customers. Sometimes new restaurants have grand opening celebrations to introduce customers to their menus. These establishments often lower their prices, give you a complete dinner for the price of an entree, or offer some other discount. Taking an entire family out for dinner can be an expensive excursion unless you are able to find a place that has children's and/or senior prices. Even many fast-food places have senior discounts.

Try a new restaurant, or one you're unfamiliar with, at lunch. Most better restaurants charge lower prices for lunch, and many offer virtually the same selection as they have for dinner.

Take advantage of coupons or other offers. Like grocery stores, restaurants often participate in advertising campaigns that offer coupons entitling you to a discount of some kind. Some restaurants will give you a free sandwich or other enticement after you have made a certain number of purchases. Other places offer two-for-one deals, which are good if you plan to share a meal with someone. If you're planning a meal out as a birthday celebration, phone around; many restaurants offer a free meal (or at least a free dessert) for birthday parties.

If you want to be considered for special prices, phone ahead and ask the manager what accommodations are available. A restaurant may not list a children's menu, for example, but may be quite willing to serve a child's portion at a lower price if asked. Our children love salads, but they cannot eat much. In restaurants with a salad bar, I always ask if there's a child's salad plate for less money. My husband and I like salad bars and often buy one meal with two salad bars and split the entree. Some restaurants serve such large portions that it makes sense to split a dinner. As long as you aren't buying an all-you-can-eat meal, the restaurant should have no problem with you asking for a second plate. Some add a small charge for this, but it is still less than buying another dinner.

  Order a complete meal rather than ordering à la carte, which is generally more expensive.

Even fast-food restaurants offer complete meals at special prices, which can be a good buy if you're hungry and like everything in the meal.

 Be thrifty with your order. There's no law that says that you have to order a beverage with dinner, for instance. In most restaurants, in terms of what you receive for your money, the beverage is the most expensive item on the menu. Ask to have your water glass refilled periodically, or simply order water. This can save calories as well as money. Some places offer pitchers of drinks for the whole party that are cheaper than ordering by the glass. Another way to save money is to skip dessert. Many of us have a tendency to order it just because it's there. Then we either stuff ourselves and feel miserable, or we leave half of the dessert on the plate. Think of the calories you can save while you're saving money. If you must order dessert, ask to have it packed "to go" so that you can eat it when you're less full and will enjoy it more.

If you order a beverage, ask for it with little or no ice. Most soft drinks are already cold enough when they're dispensed. If you get a glass half filled with ice, which is typical, you're paying half of the price of the beverage for water.

If you have substantial amounts of leftover food, ask for carry-out packaging. You're paying for the food, so if you have leftovers and if you're going straight home, saving part of a meal is your prerogative.

Tip only for good service. At most restaurants, it's customary to tip your server, with the standard amount (depending on the kind of restaurant, the number of people in your group, and other factors) being about 15 percent of the total bill. A "TIP" should mean "To Insure Promptness," and if you receive extremely slow or surly service, you shouldn't feel guilty about not leaving a tip.

OTHER LEISURE ACTIVITIES

Many different leisure activities vie for your limited dollars. Movies, concerts, sporting events, bowling, the theater—and many other educational and entertaining pastimes too numerous to list—clamor for your attention. While how you use your leisure time is certainly your own business, don't overlook activities in which you can participate rather than be a spectator—usually, the greater the degree of participation, the better. In general, the more you participate in an activity, the more rewarding it will be. Thus, while watching television is okay, reading, jogging, and visiting the zoo are better. Seeing a movie can be fun, but learning to act in your community theater could be even more fun, with the added bonus that you're learning a meaningful hobby.

Very often, you can combine several different goals: have fun, learn a great deal, exercise your mind and body—and save money in the process. Sometimes you can even turn a leisure activity—such as woodworking or knitting—into a money-making venture. (Before you try this, however, check to see if there are any licensing, zoning, or other restrictions or requirements that might apply in your area. It's better to find this out before you start than to face a fine later.)

Whatever you decide to do with your leisure time, there are some ways to spend less, and I want to mention just a few.

If you like to go to the movies, go to a matinee, or look for small theaters that charge less because they get the movies several months after they have opened elsewhere. You won't see the movie as soon, but the price is sometimes half (or less) of the regular, first-run price.

If they're available in your area, attend drive-in movies. Drive-ins are a terrific (although rapidly vanishing) alternative for families with small children. You can see the movie on a large screen, bring your own snacks, and if the children get tired, they can sleep. Many drive-ins have double features so you really can enjoy a bargain.

If you have a videocassette recorder (VCR), rent a movie and watch it at home. There are so many video rental outlets that you can always find a special promotional price if you search hard enough. You can watch at your convenience, provide your own snacks, and put tired children to bed. Remember, you can extend the life of your VCR if you invest in a cassette rewinder for your tapes.

Instead of spending large sums of money watching professional sports, join a community softball, soccer, bowling—or whatever suits your style—team. You'll have more fun, meet new people, and gain in physical fitness, too.

Become active in a community theater group. If you don't care to act, manage the lighting or sound system, or help build the sets. The costs to you will be negligible, and the rewards may far surpass your expectations. Similarly, many local churches and schools have orchestras, choruses, and bands that may provide an enjoyable time for little or no cost, whether you actually sing or play an instrument, or merely provide moral support.

If you live near a large city, you might be able to buy discount theater tickets by going to the box office or discount ticket outlet shortly before the performance starts. If you frequently attend live entertainment that has a "season," you and one or more friends may be able to buy a season ticket that saves money over the individual performance price, and then share it, rotating who will go to the event on which date. An added bonus is that sometimes buying a season ticket means receiving one of the best seats in the house.

Compare the price of advance tickets to that of the same tickets bought at the door. Often tickets are cheaper if you buy them ahead of time.

Visit a museum or zoo. Museums, once looked upon as being stodgy and boring, have plenty of life now. Modern technology and creative thinking are providing stimulating exhibits that interest people of all ages. Many museums across the country are designed especially for children, with "hands-on" exhibits that are touchable. The San Francisco Exploratorium and the New York Hall of Science are two examples, but such fun-filled places now exist all over the country. If you visit a museum often, in many cases you can purchase a membership and save money on the price of admission, receive discounts in the gift shop, and sometimes be placed on a mailing list to receive information regarding upcoming events. Similar memberships at zoos are usually available also. For pure enjoyment, and education besides, nothing can top the value of a visit to a museum or zoo.

Take advantage of the services offered by your public library. Today's libraries not only have books and periodicals, but also records, audio- and video-tapes, compact discs—even artwork by local artists. Some libraries offer special services such as story time for small children, adult discussion groups and educational programs, or mobile library service for outlying areas. You can request that a specific book be held for you; when it comes in, you can pick it up at your library or ask that it be sent out on the mobile unit when it's near your house. The current newspapers and magazines found in your local library are not only a source of valuable information but they provide enjoyable reading as well. And best of all, these services are available free or for a very small charge!

Entertain friends and family. An important, relatively inexpensive part of leisure time should consist of entertaining your friends and family. I, for one, believe it is time to revive the nearly lost art of socializing. Social occasions can be as simple as inviting a friend or two for a quiet evening, or as complicated as a wedding reception. Children also enjoy entertaining their friends.

Keep your entertaining as inexpensive as you want it to be. The cost-conscious host or hostess has many options available to insure a good time at a minimal cost. Clubs and other large groups can throw a fun party by having a progressive dinner party, in which the group eats one course of the meal at one home, then moves on to the next individual's home for another course, and so on. Another inexpensive type of dinner party is a "potluck" dinner, to which everyone brings a favorite dish. If many people in your extended family or group of friends have a birthday in the same month, a collective birthday party is an option. That way, one cake and one set of party favors can serve for several people.

Cakes can be an expensive element of any party. For a wedding, consider buying a sheet cake instead of one of the multi-tiered variety. You can usually save 60 to 70 percent of the cost, the cake is easier to cut, and less is likely to be wasted. Sheet cakes are good for children's parties also; it's difficult to cut a sliver of layer cake for a small diner who can't eat that much. Or try making your own cakes. This will save you lots of money compared to buying them from the grocery store or bakery. And there are easy ways to make a homemade cake look as special as the store-bought variety, even if you don't think of yourself as artistic. Use cookie cutters to make outlines on the frosting, and then fill in the shapes with colored icing. Or try decorating a cake with cookies. A round layer cake can be turned into a merry-go-round with the addition of a few animal crackers and a little bit of frosting or licorice laces. For a small child's birthday cake, use 3D plastic puzzle pieces as decoration. The puzzle can then be used after the party. You can also decorate cakes by sprinkling colored or white powdered sugar through a doily or stencil that has been laid on top of the frosting. If you're more ambitious, you can take a conventional sheet cake, cut it up and fit the pieces together and then frost the cake in a new shape that fits the occasion, such as a heart, a four-leaf clover, or an Easter bunny. (Baker's Coconut has had a book out for as long as I can remember that offers instructions for this technique.)

If you want to capture some of your leisure activities for posterity, select the ways and means carefully. If you want an event like a wedding recorded on videocassette, for example, instead of hiring a professional you can usually find a friend do it for you. The proficiency of your friend will affect your decision, of course, and you may want to provide him or her with an extra videotape to practice with before the actual event. Similarly, if you aren't good at taking photographs, you can almost always find an amateur shutterbug among your friends who is willing to help out. The charge for developing photographs is the most expensive part of taking pictures. Instant film is the most expensive and should be used sparingly, unless you absolutely must see the results immediately. You can get good quality developing for reasonable prices if you send your film away to be developed. It takes about two weeks, but the savings can be well worth the wait. Check around for developing specials when you can get two prints for the price of one, or bigger prints for the regular price.

If shopping and buying gifts are a big part of your leisure fun, reconsider your thinking. If you're trying to pinch pennies, it's simply best to avoid "recreational shopping." Not all gifts need to be material things, and the value of a gift is not necessarily reflected in its cost. Remember, not all gifts can be touched right away; helping someone with a move and baby-sitting for a friend are intangible, but usually most appreciated. A coupon book filled with services you'll render during the year makes a thoughtful birthday gift. An offer to cook for someone who's ill or who has just had a baby is "touchable," but in the future. By being imaginative you can give very special gifts at a minimal cost. In most cases, a special gift of caring or doing a kindness for someone will be remembered and appreciated far longer than a purchased trinket. If you exchange gifts with another person regularly, you can make it interesting by setting limits and changing the requirements as needed. For instance, specify no gifts costing over five dollars, baked goods only, or something homemade.

Try to spread your gift shopping out over the course of the year, taking advantage of sales when possible. If you see something that will fit one of your future gift needs and it's on sale, buy it. Spreading out these purchases will help you avoid massive charging sprees later. This is also a helpful idea for parents of small children who let them know at the last minute about the birthday party they've been invited to . . . tomorrow.

If the person you need a gift for is hard to buy for, consider buying a gift certificate at a store you know he or she shops at. If the recipient is a smart shopper, he or she may be able to use it to buy something on sale, and if you're mailing the gift, a certificate requires less postage than a package. And it will cut down on your shopping time—and the temptation to impulse buy while you're looking for a gift.

  Stock up on gift wrap, cards, and other holiday items in advance. Most stores sell holiday-related merchandise at half price immediately after the holiday; take advantage of this and you'll not only save money, you'll save yourself from doing some frantic shopping when the holiday rolls around.

If you send a lot of cards, look into boxed assortments. Often you can save at least 50 percent of the price of the cards if you buy them in boxes rather than individually.

Buy all-occasion assortments of gift wrap instead of specialized patterns. You can also save on gift wrap by recycling the wrapping paper from large gifts and using it to wrap smaller gifts. Another alternative to expensive wrapping paper is to use the comic pages from the newspaper to wrap your gifts. This works really well for children's gifts. For adults, you might want to use the sports page or the financial section instead.

Regardless of what some may say, I believe Americans work harder than any other people in the world. Many Americans still play hard also, but I'm afraid we're fast becoming a nation of "couch potatoes" who celebrate our leisure time by stuffing ourselves as we watch someone else perform for us. Perhaps the main reason we glorify athletes, actors, and other performers, and why we tolerate paying them such outrageous salaries, is that we feel guilty because we're not doing more with our leisure time.

The *American Heritage Dictionary* defines *leisure* as "freedom from time-consuming duties, responsibilities, or activities." Notice that nowhere in this definition is it implied that you must sit and passively do little or nothing. Quite to the contrary, leisure time is *your* time rather than your employer's time, time in which you have the *freedom* to do as you please. Does it make sense to waste your time? And does it make sense to spend more of your hard-earned money than you have to in order to pay for your leisure? After all, you have already worked and earned your leisure time, so why should you pay for it again? Of course, you can *choose* to spend money on leisure activities that bring you pleasure. But just remember: Think deliberately about your choices, weigh them carefully, and don't spend your leisure time unprofitably.

10

Saving Money on Your Health

Pause for a moment and reflect on the double paradox involving your health if you live in the United States of America. Most people would probably agree that almost nothing is more important than their health. Without good health, things like the kind of car you drive, what your clothes look like, or how much money you earn aren't very meaningful. And the state of medical awareness in the United States surpasses that of anywhere else in the world. We now know what causes most diseases, and in many instances we know what we can do to prevent them or at least lessen their effects. Yet incredibly, although good health is undeniably our most prized possession, and although we are informed regarding the consequences to our health, many people still refuse to take care of themselves or, even worse, they abuse their bodies and minds on a daily basis. This first paradox—that people maltreat their most valuable possession—never ceases to amaze me, and every time I witness individuals abusing their bodies, I want to cry out and stop them.

The second paradox concerns affordable health care, a major concern for the majority of Americans. Our nation, with all its great accomplishments, is one of the few successful democracies that has not been able to provide health care for all its citizens. Indeed, health care costs are skyrocketing out of control for most of us, and even if you are fortunate enough to have health insurance, a major accident or illness can still be financially devastating. This second paradox—that the richest and most technologically advanced nation in the world, the country with more doctors and medical facilities than any other, is unable to adequately take care of all its sick and injured—is bewildering, and also frightening. President Clinton has made the overhauling of our health care system a top priority of his administration, and a variety of health plans have been proposed for our nation by medical professionals and politicians. Until they can come to an agreement on some kind of affordable, comprehensive medical care, however, and until it becomes available, most consumers must fend for themselves.

One way you can fend for yourself is to find an employer who is willing and able to pay for your health insurance. Thus, when you are searching for a new job or negotiating your salary, the availability of medical benefits must be a primary concern. However, most small companies, since they rarely qualify for group plans, find it overwhelmingly expensive to provide adequate health care for their employees. If you can't secure health insurance through an employer, you may be able to become part of a group plan through a club, fraternal organization, or other group. Individuals can purchase health insurance on their own, of course, but the fact is that most people simply cannot afford it. As a penny-wise consumer, you can look for ways to save on your medical costs, such as alternative medical care, cheaper insurance, and lower-priced drugs. And perhaps the best financial defense of all is to try your best to stay healthy and to avoid accidents.

STAYING HEALTHY

The best way to avoid medical bills is to stay as healthy and accident-free as possible. Obviously you can't control your genetic composition, and neither can you avoid every virus or bacterium that's around. There are times that you'll get sick or have an accident, but here are some things you can do to maximize your control over your health and minimize your health-related bills.

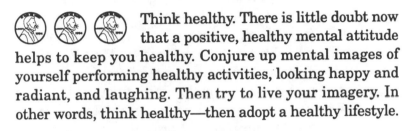 Think healthy. There is little doubt now that a positive, healthy mental attitude helps to keep you healthy. Conjure up mental images of yourself performing healthy activities, looking happy and radiant, and laughing. Then try to live your imagery. In other words, think healthy—then adopt a healthy lifestyle.

When you do come down with an illness, reassert your positive attitude as soon as possible. The more you can smile, laugh, and get yourself back to doing healthy things, the faster you will recover. (Of course, depending on the illness, your body requires time to rest and restore itself to health, so don't rush it too much.)

Eat healthy. A good diet is an essential ingredient of a healthy lifestyle, and it costs no more to eat wholesome foods than it does to eat junk. In fact, in most cases you'll actually save money by eating more vegetables and fruit, more cereals and bread, and less meat, fat, sugar, and processed foods. The media are filled with advice on nutrition, and sometimes it can be confusing. One fact is certain, though: Research shows that a healthy diet can help you feel better and live longer.

Focus on eating whole, fresh foods, with as much fiber and as little fat, salt, and other additives as you can. Find out how to improve your eating habits, save money, and enjoy your new vitality. It's well worth the effort!

Develop a regular exercise program. It doesn't have to be fancy, costly, or painful. What is important is that you exercise regularly, preferably every day. Depending on your age and overall health, your program could include swimming, dancing, bowling, golf, tennis, jogging, and many other fun-filled activities. Even walking briskly for thirty minutes at least four times a week significantly lowers your risk of developing heart disease and osteoporosis. You'll find that you rest and eat better when on a regular exercise program, too, which is important because your body is more susceptible to illness when you're run down.

As much as possible, avoid stressful situations. Too much stress can lower the body's resistance to diseases of all kinds. Continued stress has been linked to stroke and heart disease especially. Even more important than avoiding stress—and obviously you cannot avoid all stress in your life—is how you *react* to the stress, that is, whether you can regain some control over your mind and body rather than allowing the stressful situation to totally control you. For instance, is being stuck in a traffic jam, perhaps being late for work, really the worst thing in the world? If you can't move your vehicle, that much is out of your control, but whether you rant and rave or use that time to think about something pleasant or puzzle out a problem or plan your day is—or should be—controlled by you.

If you smoke or otherwise use tobacco, stop. You'll save the hundreds of dollars a year you're paying for a product that's harming your health, you'll feel better, and you may just save your life, too.

Depending on your age and overall health, have a complete physical periodically. While a thorough physical is expensive, many of today's illnesses can be cured or alleviated if discovered soon enough. Your goal is to reduce the cost of your health care but not at the expense of your health. Get to know your own body. If something changes or doesn't seem right to you, you can alert your doctor and possibly catch an illness early.

Prevent tooth decay by brushing your teeth after meals and flossing regularly. If you eat all day long, your odds of getting cavities are higher because tooth decay gets its best chance within the first twenty minutes after you eat. Flossing helps prevent gum disease, bone loss, and the need for root canal surgery.

Have regular dental checkups. See your dentist regularly so you can catch problems when they're small, before you need major dental procedures.

Unless a doctor has advised you to take vitamin and mineral supplements, be cautious in what you take. Buying bottles of supplements can be very expensive. Megadoses of supplements may not do you any good and, in some cases, can be dangerous to your health.

Protect yourself from environmental health hazards. An important part of staying healthy and reducing your health-related expenses is protecting yourself from hazards like too much sun, exposure to asbestos, secondhand smoke, and other potentially damaging environmental factors. Protecting yourself from the sun is one of the easiest things to do. When you go out in the sun, wear a hat with a wide brim, sunglasses (get ones that filter out both UVA and UVB rays), and a sunblock with a sun protection factor (SPF) of 15 or higher. Small children can be protected with less sunblock if you dress them in oversized T-shirts.

Food Safety

Although we all make jokes about the strange things growing in the refrigerator, spoiled food is no laughing matter. Taking a chance on making yourself or someone else sick is not worth the few pennies you might save using leftover food. If you're in doubt about how long food has been in the fridge, by all means throw it out. If you use common sense, though, and bear in mind the following tips, there's no reason you can't make the most of your food (see Chapter 3, Reducing Your Grocery Bill) and remain healthy, too.

If you're participating in a picnic or a buffet, control the temperature of your dish. If your dish is meant to be served hot, try to maintain a temperature over 140°F. If it's meant to be served cold, it should be kept under 45°F. When you've finished eating, clear the table and put perishables in the refrigerator. Food that's kept sitting out longer than two hours without temperature control is questionable and should be thrown out.

When you prepare food, wash your hands thoroughly and bandage any cuts to keep bacteria from contaminating your food. Wash all foods, including vegetables, thoroughly. If you're using a single cutting board to prepare meat as well as vegetables that will be eaten raw, cut the vegetables first. If there are any bacteria in the meat, they will likely be killed by cooking until the internal temperature reaches 200°F, but if you contaminate the vegetables by having them come in contact with uncooked meat drippings, and then eat the vegetables raw or undercooked, you're asking for trouble. Similarly, don't allow meat to be packed in the same container as vegetables that are going to be eaten raw. Don't let juice from raw meat contaminate your cooked meats, either, and never use the same dish for serving cooked meat that was used previously to store or carry raw meat. Use these same precautions in handling raw poultry and eggs.

Thaw meat and other perishables in the refrigerator rather than on your counter to limit bacterial growth. Once a product is thawed, don't refreeze it unless you cook it first.

Cook all meats thoroughly to make sure they're safe to eat. Some foods are no longer safe to eat raw. In much of the United States, salmonella poisoning (from various strains of *Salmonella* bacteria) has reached nearly epidemic proportions. Do not eat raw eggs (or sauces prepared with raw eggs), raw seafood, or raw or undercooked meat of any kind. You may prefer your meat extra rare, but to eat it that way is to risk illness and an expensive visit to the doctor.

Preventing Accidents

Staying healthy also means preventing accidents, many of which can occur right in your own home. Take some time to look around your home for potential hazards. Many dangerous situations can be corrected quickly and economically. Remember, it's always less expensive to take precautionary measures than to wait until after an accident has occurred. Then you'll still have to correct the problem that caused the accident, but in addition you could be confronted with exorbitant medical bills, lost pay, or even a lawsuit.

If you have children, or if children visit your home often, try to change your perspective to be aware of hazards for little people. Look at your home from a child's level and try to notice the attractive dangers that stand out. Whereas as adults we hardly notice electrical outlets, for example, if you're a little person whose eyes are close to the level of the outlets, they become much more inviting. No wonder children are constantly tempted to stick their fingers or small objects into the electrical outlets! I'll begin with a few suggestions about preventing accidents involving children, and then I'll mention some things you can do to prevent adults from having accidents, too.

  Cover electrical outlets to prevent kids from sticking things (and fingers) into them. There are a variety of outlet covers available, including some that will cover an outlet that has cords plugged into it. This will prevent kids from pulling plugs and trying to put them back in.

Don't leave appliances plugged in when not in use. Kids figure out how to turn on even the most complicated switches, and the result could be disaster. An unplugged appliance with a cord that is left hanging off the edge of the counter is an open invitation for a small child to pull on it.

Keep small and breakable objects out of a child's reach. You may think a potential hazard is up high enough, but small kids have those elastic, suction-cup fingers that can reach farther than you realize. Most small objects will immediately be put into a young child's mouth and present a choking hazard. If you're unsure as to whether an item is small enough for a child to choke on, it is! Surprisingly, anything smaller than a television set seems to fit into a child's mouth.

Keep all medicines, cosmetics, cleaning supplies, and any other potentially dangerous chemicals locked up and up high—not under the kitchen sink. After children are big enough to move around with ease, keep the key hidden also. One way to lock up these items is to buy child-resistant locks and latches. Remember to keep an eye on dangerous chemicals when you're using them, too. Most inadvertent poisonings occur while the substance is being used.

Keep pot or pan handles turned inward when you are cooking something on the stove. Children can easily grab handles that are turned outward and scald themselves.

If you have a baby in a crib, make sure you keep the crib away from drawstrings for curtains, drapes, or blinds. A child can play with the drawstring and possibly strangle himself. If a child's bed must be near a drawstring, secure it so that it is out of the child's reach.

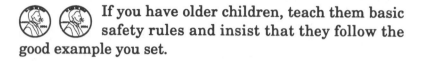 If you have older children, teach them basic safety rules and insist that they follow the good example you set.

If your child rides a bicycle, buy a helmet and require him or her to wear it. Many children are seriously hurt each year because their heads are not protected. Check your pediatrician's office for coupons for bicycle helmets. Some companies that sell products for children also offer discount coupons for bicycle helmets.

Use an approved child restraint when transporting your precious cargo. Most states require child restraints in automobiles. If you have a child who requires a special child's car seat, it should travel *everywhere* with you—starting with the ride home from the hospital. If you're flying, your child can use it on the plane or you can check it as baggage, but it must come with you. Always wear your seat belt and insist that your passengers do the same. Children will develop the habit of using seat belts if they know they're expected to use them and if they see adults setting an example.

Learn to scrutinize your workspace and living area for potential hazards. Most accidents are preventable, if only you could see into the future and realize what was about to occur. Train yourself to think analytically, seeing each commonplace object or situation as a potential hazard and how it could cause an accident, and you can then remove or lessen the potential for trouble. If you have small throw rugs in your home, for example, picture yourself or a loved one stretched out on the floor with a broken arm or leg. Once you have visualized this potential problem, you are more likely to make sure the rugs have a slip-resistant backing. Showers and bathtubs are also places where people slip easily. Visualize the predicament if you or your spouse slipped and were knocked unconscious, lying there in your otherwise empty house, needing help. Such accidents occur every day, of course, but always—you believe—to someone else. The trick to preventing most accidents is *convincing yourself that it can happen to you.* Whatever you're doing, take your time, be cautious, and concentrate on the task at hand.

   If you're working with power tools, make sure all the pieces are secure before starting the tool. Remember to use the right tool for the job. (Picture the tool flying apart in your face.) When you use a power lawn mower, wear sturdy shoes and check the cutting area for rocks, small toys, or other debris that you could hit. Children should not be permitted to be in the area when you are operating a lawn mower. (Picture a small child injured by a piece of rock.) Make sure appliances are unplugged before you work on them, and turn off the circuit breaker or remove the fuse for that area if you're working on wiring, light fixtures, ceiling fans, etc. (Picture yourself on the floor, shocked and unable to call for help.)

Learn basic first aid techniques and teach them to other members of your family. The Red Cross offers classes including demonstrations of cardiopulmonary resuscitation (CPR). You should also know the Heimlich maneuver for choking emergencies. The more quickly these procedures are done, the less damage to the victim.

Note: CPR must be taught by a certified instructor.

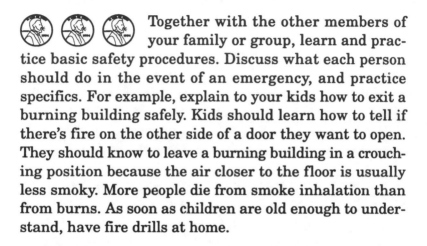 Together with the other members of your family or group, learn and practice basic safety procedures. Discuss what each person should do in the event of an emergency, and practice specifics. For example, explain to your kids how to exit a burning building safely. Kids should learn how to tell if there's fire on the other side of a door they want to open. They should know to leave a burning building in a crouching position because the air closer to the floor is usually less smoky. More people die from smoke inhalation than from burns. As soon as children are old enough to understand, have fire drills at home.

HEALTH INSURANCE

No matter how hard you try to stay healthy and prevent accidents, in all probability sooner or later you will require medical care. As we all know, health care costs are increasing at alarming rates. If your employer does not provide you with a group plan, and pay most of the premium, you—along with many other Americans—are faced with a dilemma. Do you purchase health insurance, which can run $300 to $400 a month for a family policy with a $500 deductible? Or do you take a chance and perhaps face financial ruin if someone has a catastrophic illness?

Certainly I would recommend that, if at all possible, you carry health insurance—even if you have to pay for all of the premiums out of your own pocket. The risks are just too great otherwise. By far your best strategy is to align yourself with an employer who pays all or most of the premium. In addition to the lower cost of a group plan through your employer, another advantage is that your premiums are deducted before your taxes are withheld, so you're gaining a significant tax break. Group insurance also generally provides a better range of benefits, at a lower unit cost, than individual policies, mainly because the insurance company's risk is spread over a large group of fairly healthy people. If you're not covered by your employer, however, try the following alternatives.

If you belong to a union, fraternal organization, auto club, credit union, or any other group, find out if members are eligible to join a group health plan. If no plan is available, talk to your colleagues and look into beginning one. Chances are, if you are not a participant in a group insurance plan, many of your friends aren't either. You may just need someone to take a leadership role in exploring the possibilities, and it might as well be you.

Contact the Blue Cross-Blue Shield office in your area and explain your predicament. The agent should be able to tell you what options you have, what regional organizations have plans, etc.

Contact your life insurance agent. Although group plans tend to be less expensive, with better coverage, this is not always the case. Your agent may be able to show you a policy that will fulfill your needs at a reasonable price.

Explore alternative health care plans in your region. For example, there may be a health maintenance organization (HMO) that you can join, usually again through a group. HMOs stress regular health care, the prevention of illness, and efficient treatment. You pay monthly premiums but only a nominal fee for office visits, although you must visit participating doctors only.

Whatever type of health policy you consider, examine the details closely. Make sure you're covered for both illness and accidental injury. Check the policy's provisions concerning renewal and cancellation, and make sure you understand what illnesses and procedures are excluded from payment. In general, you are better off having one comprehensive policy rather than several policies with restricted coverage. Most individual health policies have a ten-day examination period during which you have the right to refuse the contract even though you have already signed it; if you find a provision in the policy that doesn't meet your needs, or if you simply don't understand some of the terminology, return the policy until you are satisfied.

If you don't already have it, consider buying disability insurance. If you suddenly become unable to work because of a major illness, you face a double whammy: high medical bills and little or no income. Disability income insurance provides for payment of your salary, or some portion of it, while you're unable to work.

 If you are eligible for Medicare but unsure about the provisions of this federal health program, ask a friend or relative to help. Many states offer free counseling services, and the U.S. Government Printing Office (telephone 202-783-3238) publishes an excellent and inexpensive *Guide to Health Insurance for People with Medicare*. Medicare does not offer complete coverage, and it may be to your advantage to subscribe to "Medigap" private health insurance to supplement, or fill the gaps not covered by, Medicare benefits.

MEDICAL CARE

No matter how healthy your lifestyle, chances are that sooner or later you and your family will require a doctor's care. If you're typical—unless you have an excellent insurance plan that covers office visits—you probably avoid or postpone seeing your doctor even if you are sick, and you seldom or never have a general checkup for preventive maintenance. In the long run, what you see as saving on doctors' fees can be more costly than visiting a doctor in a timely manner, and you should investigate ways of obtaining regular and competent medical care. It almost always costs less to treat medical problems sooner rather than later. If possible, establish a relationship with a doctor or clinic so that your own and your family's medical history can be in one place and readily accessible; that way, you can receive more personalized attention. Try to find a physician before you run into an emergency.

Whether your visit is for a routine checkup or an immediate problem, you should be able to *talk* to your doctor— no one knows better than you what you need or where something hurts. If your doctor doesn't pay attention to what you're saying, belittles you, or comments on your great physique, look for another doctor. The doctor's mind is not on what's best for you, and he or she could easily miss important details that could affect your health later on.

When I was in the military, for example, I was sent to the base clinic several times over the course of a month for symptoms of dizziness and difficulty breathing and swallowing. A blood test was taken, but the doctor who took it never followed up on it, and then told me the illness was all in my head. I didn't find out what was wrong until I was admitted to the emergency room and hospitalized with a spleen that was near the bursting point. Finally, someone looked at my records and found the blood test that had been done a week earlier (and gave a diagnosis of mononucleosis).

Most of my experiences with doctors have been quite positive since that episode, because now I always take steps to become actively involved in my treatment and call back to find out the results of any tests done. Once you're under medical care, there are some things you can do to insure adequate care at a reasonable price, also. The following are some things to keep in mind when you make your next trip to a doctor's office or clinic.

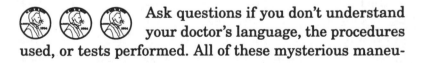 Give your doctor the most complete information possible about your medical history and symptoms, including a description of *any* drugs you're currently taking, no matter how minor they may seem. Even something as "harmless" as a daily aspirin or antacid can make a difference. Try to keep an accurate medical history to facilitate your care and to aid the doctor in his or her diagnosis.

Ask questions if you don't understand your doctor's language, the procedures used, or tests performed. All of these mysterious maneuvers cost money, and it's your body, so you have the right to know what's happening. A good doctor will be willing to discuss medical procedures, and if you are assertive but not demanding, should be eager to communicate openly with you, the patient. The more informed you are, and the more effectively you participate in the treatment, the sooner you will be well and the sooner the bills will stop.

If you are advised to use a drug that you haven't taken before, ask your doctor for free samples. If it turns out that your system won't tolerate the drug, you will not have wasted money on a prescription that you can't use.

Shop around and compare prices on medicines. Independent pharmacies are usually more expensive than the chain stores, but not always.

When you have a prescription filled, always count the number of pills dispensed before you take the package home. If the pharmacist has given you an incorrect quantity, politely point this out and request a correction. After all, you're paying for the medication, so you should make sure you get as much as you pay for.

When you're required to take medication, make sure you follow all instructions, no matter how minor they seem. Eating or not eating with your medicine can make a difference in its effectiveness, as can the timing of the dosage. And discontinuing antibiotics before you have taken the prescribed amount—even though you're feeling better—can allow bacteria another chance to overwhelm your immune system. Plus, the bacteria can become resistant to the antibiotic, rendering the medicine ineffective the next time it is administered.

Avoid overmedicating yourself. Most prescription medicines are very powerful drugs. If you're under a doctor's care and you're given a new prescription, make sure the doctor knows what other medications you're already taking, even if the previous illness is unrelated to your current complaint. An incompatible mixture of drugs can cause your medications to be ineffective at best and lethal at worst. If in doubt about a particular combination of over-the-counter medicines, ask your pharmacist. Even over-the-counter drugs are very expensive, and in many cases you would be better off, and save time and money, if you skipped the self-prescribed medication and allowed your body to rest and heal itself.

Don't store your medicines in the bathroom. The moisture and germs in the bathroom can cause the medicine to deteriorate, requiring you to purchase additional drugs.

Throw out all medicines that have passed their expiration dates. Some medicines, like codeine, become more potent with age, while others have a diminished effectiveness and would be useless when you really need them. Taking out-of-date medicine in a mistaken attempt to save money could cost you a great deal more in the long run.

Ask your doctor if there is a suitable generic equivalent for your prescription. If so, you could possibly save 25 to 50 percent of the price of the higher priced drug. Sometimes substitution is not possible (you may need a timed-release medication and the generic product may not be a timed-release form, for example), but you won't know if you don't ask. Also, if you refill a prescription and you notice that the medication looks different than it did last time, ask your pharmacist about it immediately. It could be a different brand. Worse, it could be a different dosage—or even the wrong medicine.

If you require a hospital stay and you're already taking medication regularly, check to see if you can take your medication with you to the hospital for the staff to administer. It's amazing how expensive even one little pill can be when the hospital supplies it.

If you're scheduled for elective surgery, ask your doctor about the advisability of storing your own blood for use during the operation. With the advent of AIDS, many people are frightened of receiving blood transfusions from unknown sources. Although all donated blood is now tested for the presence of infectious disease agents, especially HIV (the virus that causes AIDS), many people are now choosing autologous blood donation (donating and storing their own blood). The advantages of this include a reduced risk of infection, a reduced chance of your body rejecting "foreign" matter, and in many instances a reduced cost.

When you go to another doctor for a second opinion, ask if you can have any relevant tests and x-rays sent to the second doctor. Besides being expensive, some of these tests can be painful, and you wouldn't want to go through them a second time unnecessarily.

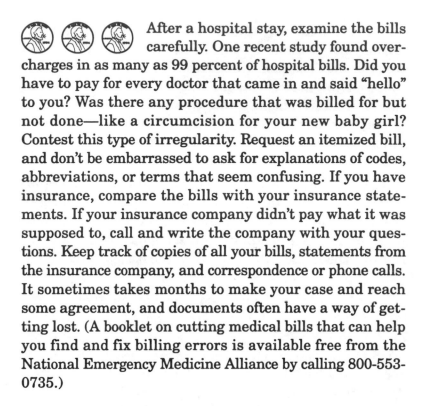 After a hospital stay, examine the bills carefully. One recent study found over- charges in as many as 99 percent of hospital bills. Did you have to pay for every doctor that came in and said "hello" to you? Was there any procedure that was billed for but not done—like a circumcision for your new baby girl? Contest this type of irregularity. Request an itemized bill, and don't be embarrassed to ask for explanations of codes, abbreviations, or terms that seem confusing. If you have insurance, compare the bills with your insurance state- ments. If your insurance company didn't pay what it was supposed to, call and write the company with your ques- tions. Keep track of copies of all your bills, statements from the insurance company, and correspondence or phone calls. It sometimes takes months to make your case and reach some agreement, and documents often have a way of get- ting lost. (A booklet on cutting medical bills that can help you find and fix billing errors is available free from the National Emergency Medicine Alliance by calling 800-553- 0735.)

Pinching pennies only makes sense if it makes it pos- sible for you to enjoy more of the things you want out of life. As I've implied, most people act as if they're going to live and be healthy forever, which is simply a wonderful dream. Fortunately, there are many steps you can take to extend your life and improve your health, prevent acci- dents, and find better and more economical medical care if it becomes necessary. Then you can truly enjoy the assets you have accumulated, and you will be a genuinely wealthy individual.

11

Pinching Pennies
as a
Way of Life

The last few years have marked a watershed in the development of our nation. For the first time in the history of the United States, young adults can no longer be assured that they will be better off financially than their parents; in fact, it now seems certain that at least the next few generations, and perhaps more, will be forced to accept the harsh reality that their lifestyles will be *diminished* in comparison to that of their parents. High unemployment, falling wages, higher costs for everything—but especially for health care and energy—these are the obstacles that seem to prevent the younger generations from attaining the American Dream of financial success.

In a very real sense, however, it is our concept of the American Dream that has gone awry. Traditionally, the American Dream promised equal opportunity for all who were willing to work hard and bide their time; the eventual reward for industriousness and patience was financial success. For some time now, though, many people have demanded these rewards without being willing to work or to wait. Our huge national debt is perhaps the most obvious symptom that our American Dream is not well, and after years of spending our future, the legacy has finally caught up with us all.

Our country has such an abundance of resources to draw on that it's sad to see the problems we have today. Our future lies before us like a treasure in a chest that has been slammed shut and padlocked; we know it's there, and we recognize its potential value, if only we could open it. Our people are the keys to unlocking the treasures that lie there, the keys to our survival. We must start at home to make it better, and then work our way outward toward the rest of the world.

As an individual who is determined to control his or her economic fate, you have already taken the first—and perhaps the hardest—step towards unlocking the chest just by reading this book. Hopefully, by now you are eager to begin pinching pennies, and to be on your way to turning pennies into dollars. If so, I challenge you now to apply the principles and tips I have presented here to your own life. Return to Chapter 1, Guidelines for Survival, and look again at the twelve guidelines I set forth. Notice that none of the twelve requires any special education or skills to put into practice. In fact, one of my chief concerns in writing this book has been that everyone—regardless of age, education, or experience—should be able to understand and use these principles; all that is required is a *desire* on your part to save money and a *willingness* to change your attitudes and habits.

Now that you have read this book and are determined to pinch pennies, you might be wondering how best to go about it. One way, of course, is to reread relevant chapters when you need the information they contain; thus, when preparing to buy a house, you would reread Chapter 5, Home Economics; when planning to purchase a car, you would reread Chapter 7, Cutting Car Costs.

Another way, though—and the one I recommend—is to

go through each chapter again carefully as soon as possible. Using a pen or marker, highlight each penny that you want to save today. Select several pennies from each chapter; then compile a list (on a separate sheet of paper, or on the back page of the book itself) of all the pennies you plan to pinch the first week. Keep a record of your savings, and total your pennies into dollars at the end of three months. Also, write down any new penny-pinching ideas you come up with, and then track their success, too. Pretty soon you'll discover that pinching pennies is not only rewarding, but it can be fun as well.

Soon you'll think twice before spending that extra dollar. You'll find yourself wondering why it took you so long to develop a budget. You'll clip coupons and plan your shopping trips to maximize your efficiency in grocery stores, restaurants, clothing stores, and everywhere else. Around the house, and in the car, you'll find yourself becoming vigilant for ways to save money and take full advantage of your other resources, such as your time, skill, and creativity. And because you realize that your health is more important even than your money, and that the best way to protect both is to take care of yourself by eating the right foods, exercising, and avoiding stressful habits, you will soon think and act healthy.

You'll see that pinching pennies is about much more than saving money; it's about changing your way of thinking. And it's about transforming your entire lifestyle. After all is said and done, you have a right to want your share of the American Dream. If you are willing to work hard and follow the strategies outlined here, the opportunity will come. And you will be ready.

Bibliography for Further Reading

Aslett, Don. *Clutter's Last Stand: It's Time to De-Junk Your Life!* Cincinnati: Writer's Digest Books, 1984.

Bear, John and Marina. *How to Repair Food.* Berkeley, CA: Ten Speed Press, 1987.

Bracken, Peg. *I Hate to Housekeep Book.* New York: Harcourt, Brace & World, 1962.

Bracken, Peg. *I Hate to Cook Book.* New York: Harcourt Brace, 1960.

Burger, Pixie, and Julia Percival. *Household Ecology.* New York: Prentice-Hall, 1971.

Campbell's Soup Company. *Creative Cooking with Soup.* New York: Beekman House, 1985.

Carcione, Joe. *The Greengrocer.* San Francisco, Chronicle Books, 1972.

Conran, Shirley. *Superwoman.* New York: Crown Publishers, 1978.

Cruse, Heloise. *Heloise All Around the House.* New York:
Prentice-Hall. 1965.

Cruse, Heloise. *Heloise's Beauty Book.* New York:
Arbor House, 1985.

Cruse, Heloise. *Heloise's Hints for the Working Woman.*
Englewood Cliffs, NJ: Prentice-Hall, 1970.

Cruse, Heloise. *Heloise's Housekeeping Hints.*
Englewood Cliffs, NJ: Prentice-Hall, 1962.

Cruse, Heloise. *Heloise's Kitchen Hints.* Englewood Cliffs,
NJ: Prentice-Hall, 1963.

Cruse, Heloise. *Heloise's Work and Money Savers.*
Englewood Cliffs, NJ: Prentice-Hall, 1967.

Cruse, Heloise. *Help! From Heloise.* New York:
Arbor House, 1981.

Cruse, Heloise. *Hints From Heloise.* New York:
Arbor House, 1980.

Diagram Group. *Child's Body (A Parent's Manual).*
New York: Paddington Press, 1977.

Diagram Group. *Man's Body (An Owner's Manual).*
New York: Paddington Press, 1977.

Diagram Group. *Woman's Body (An Owner's Manual).*
New York: Paddington Press, 1977.

Ferm, Max and Betty. *How to Save Dollars with Generic Drugs*. New York: William Morrow, 1985.

Fuchs, Nan Kathryn. *The Nutrition Detective*. Los Angeles: J.P. Tarcher, 1985.

General Foods. *Baker's Cut-Up Cake Party Book*. White Plains, NY: General Foods Corp., 1973.

German, Don and Joan. *Ninety Days to Financial Fitness*. New York: Macmillan, 1986.

Goldbeck, Nikki and David. *The Supermarket Handbook: Access to Whole Foods*. New York: New American Library, 1976.

Gore, Michael. *Encyclopedia of Household Hints and Dollar Stretchers*. Garden City, NY: Doubleday, 1977.

Graedon, Joe. *The New People's Pharmacy*. New York: Bantam/Graedon Enterprise, 1985.

Habeeb, Virginia. *Ladies' Home Journal Art of Homemaking*. New York: Simon and Schuster, 1973.

Harkness, Richard. *Drug Interaction Handbook*. Englewood Cliffs, NJ: Prentice-Hall, 1984.

Harris, Ben. *Kitchen Tricks*. Gramercy, NY: Crown Publishers, 1975.

Hillman, Howard. *Kitchen Science*. Boston: Houghton Mifflin Co., 1981.

Houseman, Bart, and Jim Webb. *The You-Don't-Need-a-Man-to-Fix-It Book*. Garden City, NY: Doubleday, 1973.

Jones, Peggy, and Pam Young. *Sidetracked Home Executives: From Pigpen to Paradise*. New York: Warner Books, 1983.

Jones, Peggy, and Pam Young. *Sidetracked Sisters Catch-up on the Kitchen*. New York: Warner Books, 1983.

Jones, Peggy, and Pam Young. *Sidetracked Sisters' Happiness File*. New York: Warner Books, 1985.

Laird, Jean E. *Around the Kitchen Like Magic*. New York: Harper & Row, 1969.

Laird, Jean E. *The Homemaker's Book of Energy Savers*. Brattleboro, VT: Stephen Greene Press, 1981.

Lansky, Vicki. *Practical Parenting Tips*. Deephaven, MN: Meadowbrook Press, 1982.

Nichols, Cicely. *The Family Formula Book*. New York: Grosset & Dunlap, 1978.

Pinkham, Mary Ellen, and Pearl Higginbotham. *Mary Ellen's Best of Helpful Hints*. New York: Warner Books/B. Lansky Books, 1979.

Porter, Sylvia. *Sylvia Porter's New Money Book for the 80's (Volumes 1 & 2)*. Garden City, NY: Doubleday, 1979.

Rachesky, Stanley. *Getting Pests to Bug Off.* New York: Crown Publishers, Inc., 1978.

Reader's Digest. *Back to Basics.* Pleasantville, NY: Reader's Digest Association, 1981.

Reader's Digest. *Complete Guide to Sewing.* Pleasantville, NY: Reader's Digest Association, 1976.

Smith, Lendon. *Feed Your Kids Right.* New York: McGraw-Hill, 1979.

Smith, Lendon. *Feed Yourself Right.* New York: McGraw-Hill, 1983.

Wallace, Dan. *The Natural Formula Book for Home and Yard.* Emmaus, PA: Rodale Press, 1982.

Index